VALEGRO

Champion Horse

VALEGRO

Champion Horse

CARL HESTER

Third Millennium
Publishing

Previous page: Carl and Valegro at home.

Right: At the KWPN Stallion Show, 's-Hertogenbosch, 2014, where Valegro was awarded the KWPN Horse of the Year title for 2013.

First published in Great Britain in 2015 by
Third Millennium Publishing, an imprint of
Profile Books Ltd
3 Holford Yard
Bevin Way
London WC1X 9HD
www.tmiltd.com

A CIP catalogue record for this book is available from The British Library.

ISBN 978 1 90899 053 2

e-ISBN 978 1 90899 073 0

Concept: Claire Hester
Co-author: Bernadette Hewitt
Lead photographer: Jon Stroud
Editor: Paul Forty
Jacket design: Steve Panton
Text design: Susan Pugsley
Picture research: Patrick Taylor

Printed and bound in Italy by L.E.G.O. SpA

CONTENTS

*At the London 2012 Olympics: Carl on Uthopia and Charlotte on
Valegro take a lap of honour after that historic team gold.*

FOREWORD

Ever since 2011, when Valegro was just starting grand prix, I've been taking
a special interest in this extraordinary horse. When I have been to Carl's
Gloucestershire yard for lessons, I have often been able to watch Valegro, Carl and
Charlotte at work together – it's such a team effort.

Having been a three-day-eventing world champion myself, I know so well the
attributes that go into making a world-class horse. My own horse Toytown has a
huge and special character. He has a place in my heart and I have memories of
him that will last for ever. Of course, to be a world champion in any equestrian
sport requires a very talented horse, both physically and mentally. Watching
Valegro work with Carl and Charlotte at home, it is easy to see that he has a
great intelligence and desire to please, which combined with an athletic body and
powerful physique have made him this outstanding dressage champion.

When Carl asked me to write this foreword, I was delighted and honoured. It
was easy to say 'yes' and to join in the accolades for Valegro. This wonderful horse
has captured my heart and imagination – just as he has for his huge number of
fans – and has reaffirmed the dedication and commitment that are required to be
truly the best in one's chosen field.

How amazing that so many of those connected with Valegro have come
together in this book to write his life story so far, with superb pictures to set the
scene. I don't know if there has ever been, or ever will be, another champion like
him, but maybe the best of all is that this glorious yet modest horse represents
Great Britain. He has made his team at home, the horse-loving British nation and
all his followers world-wide so enormously proud of him.

Zara Phillips MBE

1 | IN THE SPOTLIGHT

Blueberry. 'Bluebs'. The Professor. Valegro is many things to many people, but the one thing all his people have in common is love for him. This amazing horse, who holds every world record in the sport of dressage, has broken not only the records of others but also his own, pushing the bar higher than any other horse before him. Together with his rider, Charlotte Dujardin, and co-owner/trainer Carl Hester, he has come closer to perfection than any other dressage horse. His career is now in full flight, and having already taken at the age of thirteen the Olympic, European and World titles, as well as the World Cup crown, he has captured the hearts not only of Britain, but of the world. He is Valegro, and this is his story.

At the time of writing, only eleven riders and eleven horses have achieved over 80 per cent at grand prix level, the first being the Dutch combination of Anky van Grunsven and Salinero in 2006. Valegro and Charlotte broke their own world record at Olympia in 2014, scoring 87.460 per cent, and beating their earlier Reem Acra FEI (International Equestrian Federation) World Cup Final score set in April that year by 0.331 per cent.

But records are only a part of it. Retaining the World Cup crown in April 2015 with a freestyle score of 94.196 per cent – almost ten points ahead of nearest rivals Edward Gal and Glock's Undercover – involved a major logistical operation because the Final was held, alongside the jumping final, in Las Vegas.

Previous page: The lap of honour at Olympia 2014, after another world record for freestyle.

Left: The team return to the stables after Valegro's landmark victory at Hagen 2012.

Above: At home he's known as Blueberry…

Far left: … or 'The Professor'.

Alan Davies *is the 'super groom' who cares for Valegro. Often it is Alan and Valegro who now get asked to do TV interviews when they arrive at shows.*

I first met Blueberry when I took him to Vidauban in the south of France for his debut at grand prix. He ended up winning four classes over the two weeks. That was five years ago now, and even then I loved taking care of him; he was uncomplicated and really friendly, which made the job so easy.

He is called Blueberry because all the youngsters that arrived with him were called after fruit and vegetables. It was lucky he got that name, as there was also a Tomato and a Parsnip!

He loves all food, especially hay, which we have to ration as he puts on weight easily. He quite often demands some different haylage instead of his special 'diet' haylage, which he can object to when he sees his neighbours getting the other stuff. He loves to dunk his haylage in a bucket of fresh water, making his own sort of 'hay tea', so I always make sure he has a bucket even if he has an automatic drinker as well.

He loves routine, and he loves to be ridden first so that he can then go in the field. And he likes to have a snooze in the afternoon. He's not really fussed about other horses, although he likes travelling with Uthopia because he is nice and quiet and will share his hay. He is also very ticklish and he hates being clipped.

Valegro is amazing to ride; you feel extremely safe on him. He always has his ears pricked, he feels powerful and forward-going, but never out of control, and he loves hacking. I hack him every morning before he works with Charlotte and Carl in the school. He loves to check out what's happening in the neighbours' farms and likes to stop and see the cows, especially when they have calves. I always chat to him: he's a great listener and will always put a smile on your face, no matter how bad a day you are having!

If he was human, he would be Ben Cohen the rugby player; a big, powerful, muscular person, but very gentle and softly spoken, with a gorgeous smile!

He is a great traveller. He always loves having a hay net to chomp on, and he loves visiting new places, except for one place in France where we went. We were stopping over near Dijon for one night on the way to a show, and when we turned up, the stables weren't very big or clean. Valegro decided he wasn't staying and marched me straight back out of the door when I tried to put him in his stable.

He has lots of colour changes in his coat throughout the seasons; in the summer he is nearly black with a hint of chestnut, but in the winter, when he is clipped, he goes a steel-blue colour.

I don't ever remember him doing anything naughty – in my eyes he never does anything wrong!

A kiss for Alan at the European Championships, Herning, 2013.

The embarkation was covered by news and TV crews (as the arrival in Las Vegas would be too) and, after a photo opportunity with the reigning World Cup jumping winner Cornet D'Amour, ridden by Switzerland's Daniel Duesser, Valegro was settled onto the plane, sharing a crate with Painted Black, the mount of Spain's Morgan Barbançon Mestre. It was very much a 'business class' flight on the Boeing 777 freighter, with plenty of leg room at just two horses to an extra-sized crate (the crates look rather like double trailers) and every attention paid to each horse's idiosyncrasies and requirements: 'Wet hay or dry, sir?' 'A little sea salt with that water?' Valegro likes to dunk his own hay, and all the horses enjoyed an ad lib supply of carrots and apples. Tim Dutta, whose company organised the whole operation, said, 'Horses are just like you and me. Some fall asleep before departure and snooze most of the way, while others start praying from the minute they take off and don't stop until they've landed! But most of them are like seasoned CEOs: they've flown so many times that they just take it all in their stride.' Valegro is one of the seasoned CEOs.

So let's start with that journey to Nevada which, for the World Cup horses travelling from Europe, started on Saturday 11 April 2015 when a Qatar Airways flight took off from Schiphol airport in the Netherlands. Estimates valued the cargo of 26 jumpers and 14 dressage horses – including Valegro – at €150 million. (What percentage of that value did Valegro represent? No one will ever know, as he will never be sold by his owners Carl, Rowena Luard and Anne Barrott. He is literally priceless.) Almost 12,000 kg of equipment on eleven pallets accompanied the horses, along with ten grooms – including Alan Davies, who is always by Valegro's side on his travels – and Dutch vet Jan-Hein Swagemakers to tend the horses on the 11 hour 20 minute flight.

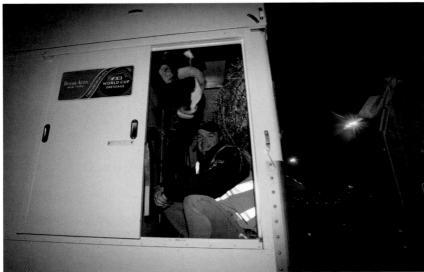

Top left: Loading up for the flight to Las Vegas.

Middle left: Alan there as ever to care for the precious cargo.

Bottom left: Onto the plane for the business class flight.

*Training at the Thomas & Mack arena
in Las Vegas – thousands watched.*

All the equipment had to be cleared through customs, and there were health checks and passport checks for the horses, followed by a short two-day period of quarantine while the blood tests were processed. Alan, along with the other grooms, had to wear white overalls for the time in quarantine, which looked a little clinical, but at least he was able to be with Valegro (grooms are not always), and there were no hitches. Charlotte flew out on the Monday, two days after Valegro, and the pair had their first exercise in the Thomas & Mack arena in Las Vegas the following day. The arena is an awkward shape, as it usually hosts concerts and sports like basketball and boxing, but a suitable equestrian arena had been constructed within it. Charlotte said with a laugh, 'It's a bit like a huge lunge-pen! I'm told it's bigger than Olympia [in London], but it doesn't feel like it – maybe it's because the seats rise so high around the ring. How are they going to fit seven judges in there?'

Spectators came in their thousands to watch the schooling sessions, applauding each of the combinations. As the riders worked in twos, Valegro and Charlotte shared the arena with El Santo and another World Cup champion, Germany's Isabell Werth. Isabell won in 1992 on Fabienne and again in 2007 on Warum Nicht, the latter in Las Vegas, and the awards stand alongside the fourteen Olympic medals in her display cabinet.

Valegro's legs were a little swollen – the bandages he wore didn't quite do the job of flight socks – and there were only a few easy days available in which to acclimatise before the competition. The team had hoped Valegro would not suffer from jet lag, but he did, as well as feeling the heat after the transition from winter weather at home to the incredible desert temperatures. Despite it all, though, and in true Valegro character, on the day of the grand prix he was ready to go.

The arena, so tight that riders had to start the test from inside the boards as there was no room to ride outside, created a very testing atmosphere for many of the field, and the enthusiastic crowd – as well as those judges that Charlotte thought wouldn't fit in – were so close. But Valegro never lets his rider down, and if Charlotte rode a little conservatively, the canter work had the true Valegro wow factor. With only a tiny loss of rhythm in the second piaffe, their score of 85 per cent was more than 5 per cent ahead of their nearest rivals. Valegro and Charlotte left the arena to a standing ovation from over 7,000 wildly cheering spectators.

Above: 'The reins slack on his neck and the sweetest expression on his face.' (Stephen Clarke.)

Top left: The Reem Acra trophy spooked many horses, but not Valegro.

Bottom left: Carl and Alan accompany Charlotte and Valegro to the arena.

Right: Charlotte's smile says it all.

Far right: A standing ovation for the 2015 FEI World Cup winners.

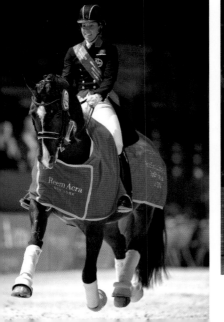

For the freestyle there was a spotlight on the new World Cup trophy created by sponsor Reem Acra. Many horses were nervous of it, but not Valegro. The US spectators totally immersed themselves in what was going on in the ring, clapping and roaring their approval not just at the end of the tests but throughout them as well. Their enthusiasm had reached fever pitch by the time the reigning champions, Valegro and Charlotte, entered the arena. If anyone was worried that the atmosphere would be difficult for Valegro, they need not have been. As Charlotte said afterwards, 'It was as if he just went, "Yahoo, I must be doing something they like!"' As ever, Valegro let Charlotte ride for tens, and she did. If he needed reassurance, he trusted her to give it to him. He went into the arena to do the job he loves, and an effortless performance ensued. To the music programme designed by Tom Hunt (using the music from the DreamWorks animated film *How to Train Your Dragon*), Valegro's elasticity in making the softest and most effortless transitions from extended canter to pirouette, his powerful yet light-footed trot extensions, his flawless piaffe and passage, and half-passes in trot and passage that float across the arena with such unrivalled expression – everything added up to another peerless performance.

The World Cup was retained by the reigning champions with a score 10 per cent higher than their nearest rivals. As Valegro walked out of the arena, so calm as Charlotte laid the reins on his neck, alternately hugging him and waving both hands to the crowd, tears welled among the cheering, whooping audience. With utter trust, and as near to perfection as the world has ever seen from a dressage horse, Valegro, as always, had given it his all.

And a few days later, after another trouble-free flight, Valegro was back in the field at home, happily engaged in his other favourite pastime, eating.

This is the story of the world's greatest dressage horse, told by his trainer and co-owner, Carl Hester, and the people who have played a part in his incredible story.

Peerless performance in the freestyle.

Clockwise from top left:

Canter pirouette;

A little reassurance from Charlotte;

Trot half-pass;

Valegro gave his all.

M ACRA FEI WORLD CUP™
DRESSAGE FINAL
LAS VEGAS 2015

Above: Total concentration for an effortless performance.

Top left: The lap of honour in Las Vegas — a standing ovation again.

Bottom left: Charlotte 'living the dream' as she accepts the new FEI World Cup dressage trophy designed by sponsor Reem Acra.

2 FROM SMALL BEGINNINGS

O n 5 July 2002 at Burgh Haamstede, an island to the south-west of Rotterdam in the Netherlands, a black/brown colt was born to a mare named Maifleur. The colt – the fourth generation through his mother's bloodline for breeders Maartje and Joop Hanse – was named Vainqueurfleur. The sire the Hanses had chosen was the promising young dressage stallion Negro. They had worked with Negro's owner, Gertjan van Olst, for years, and they told him that if the product of the match was a colt they'd let him know.

Turned loose in the long grass, the colt showed himself well, and Gertjan duly bought him. Renamed Valegro, as the van Olsts already had another horse named Vainqueurfleur, he was brought up with a view to getting him to the KWPN – the Studbook of the Royal Dutch Sport Horse – stallion grading.

Previous page: 'I remember being wildly impressed by Valegro in a young horse class but saying to Carl, "Good luck collecting that canter." ' (Stephen Clarke)

Above: A champion is born – Valegro with his dam, Maifleur, on 5 July 2002.

Left: Maartje and Joop Hanse, the proud breeders of Valegro.

Right: Gertjan van Olst with his wife Anne, key figures in Valegro's story.

Gertjan van Olst *is a renowned Dutch stallion owner and manager. His wife Anne has represented Denmark on numerous Olympic, World and European teams. Both are longstanding friends of Carl. Gertjan spotted Valegro as a foal after being invited to view him by long-term clients and small-time breeders Maartje and Joop Hanse.*

The Hanses had been clients of mine since the early 1980s, and they bred their mare Maifleur to Negro. Maifleur was a beautiful mare and Valegro was a late foal, so always one of the smaller ones in the group in the beginning. Nevertheless he always had this very strong back end, very good 'mechanics' and a really nice hind leg, but with unbelievable power in his back. Nowadays when you see him go forward and back within the pace like an accordion, that's where it comes from.

The first time I saw him, his movement was already 'tick-tock' in rhythm, which was very nice and quite rare. We raised him from about a yearling to get him ready for the KWPN stallion show. He was a classical type, and as such a small percentage get through the grading it was a reasonable decision not to take him – completely understandable. He was just not enough of a stallion. He had very normal legs, and although nowadays we know this is good for piaffe-passage, at that time they wanted long legs, and the neck high and out in front.

Carl came with us to the stallion show and liked Valegro, so he was gelded and sold to Carl. After a while Carl thought he had too many horses, so brought him back with a view to selling him. Anne's girls were riding him, and she was watching his progress, and although we had a buyer we suggested to Carl – even though I know he thought Valegro was too small – that this one had potential and it was worth spending more time on him.

Valegro was always so cooperative, always sharp, but in a very nice way, and he was always so clever, never jumpy or doing stupid things to get himself into trouble, just a really good character. And now he has such unbelievable control over his body: he wants to do his job. He's exactly what we want in a dressage horse – but how often will a horse like him come around?

I'd been training with Gertjan's wife Anne, the Danish international rider and a great friend of mine, for a while, and when I was in Holland with Escapado on one trip in January 2005 she suggested I accompany her to the KWPN stallion show and grading at Ermelo in the north of the country. As Gertjan is a well-known producer of jumping and dressage stallions and Anne was riding the black stallion Negro, a horse I really admired, I went along.

The grading was an eye-opener. The two-year-olds are each turned loose in the arena to show their paces before being sent down a jumping lane, and then a snap decision is made as to whether the horse goes forward to the next stage or not. Gertjan always presents a group of youngsters, and maybe one gets through. The rest are sold as riding horses. There was one in this group that I liked for some reason, even though he was slightly unprepossessing and 'old-fashioned' in type. As I've said elsewhere, he had 'the head of a duchess and the bottom of a cook'. He certainly wasn't flashy, and he was small, but he was strong, and he had a great canter and a great attitude. And he wasn't expensive, so I made the decision to buy him. That youngster was Valegro, and after he had been gelded, he came to England.

At the age of three-and-a-half, he went up to my neighbour Sandra Biddlecombe's yard to be backed. Sandra is great with the youngsters and has started a lot of babies off for me over the years. Valegro never put a foot wrong. He had a cobby trot and a nice walk, but this very good canter and outlook. But by the time he was four he was only sixteen hands and rather squat, and as I thought he'd never be big enough for me I called Suzanne Davies, a friend who trained with me, and offered Valegro to her. I got a yes over the phone, but a week later poor Suzanne got a tax bill and rang me back to say she couldn't afford him after all!

It wasn't a problem, as I was about to go to a show in Holland, so I decided I'd take Valegro back to Anne van Olst for her to sell him for me. But after a few days I got a call from Anne and Gertjan to say that this one would be good and I should keep him. So back came Valegro to my yard in Gloucestershire once more.

Above: Valegro's sire, Negro (Ferro x Fewrie). Himself a champion, Negro has power in the hindleg, which he passes to his offspring.

Left: Joop Hanse with Maifleur at home in Holland.

Top: Weidyfleur, Maifleur's dam, who won many championships.

Middle: Valegro, already changing colour, at one month old in the field with his mother.

Bottom: Valegro's first time in the field, with Maartje Hanse and Maifleur.

Sandra Biddlecombe *(pictured above) takes most of Carl's youngsters for breaking in. A near neighbour to his yard in Gloucestershire, she is an integral part of the Hester set-up.*

Valegro was a funny little thing really; not long-legged – he looked rather like a typical Irish horse. He had this beautiful expression, and all he wanted to do was work. He was so brave from the start, a lovely person.

Bryony, my nephew's wife, was the first to lean over him. We always do that in the stable first, and he'd been prepared, having gone through the stallion grading, so he knew about lungeing and so on. He had a fantastic walk and a huge canter – you felt you wouldn't keep up with him. Looking back, I'd never thought 'wow'; rather, what a very active mover. From the off, he was as honest as the day is long, and so easy, with a fantastic mind. He'd go down the road as brave as anything, never looking at things except out of interest.

He had a break at Carl's, then we had him back to start him again. He'd been in the paddock and carved out a trench, so that tail was like a huge ball of mud – it took ages to get off!

I could cry that he's come all this way. Charlotte has horses here, and if I see her and Valegro out I'll give him a sugar cube and feel, as we all do here, so lucky to have been part of his journey.

Joop and Maartje Hanse started breeding with the Royal Dutch Warmblood (KWPN) mare Petite Fleur. She was a very good mover, as were as her offspring. She was Valegro's great grand-dam and rather a character, and she was quite 'hot' too. Her first foal was to prove her most important; Weidyfleur, a beautiful chestnut filly who won championship after championship until the Hanses decided not to show her in breeding classes any more as she had proven herself. She had eight foals, one of which was Maifleur, the only one the Hanses kept. Maifleur too was a winner in breed classes, and is still in happy retirement with her owners, having produced that other winner, Valegro. The story shows the patience needed by successful breeders. Four generations after their purchase of the foundation mare, and after years of carefully making combinations with the right stallions for their mares, a very happy colt foal by Negro was born.

Valegro was born on 5 July 2002. He looked like all our other foals. Over thirty years of breeding we have bred around fifty foals, and we're always happy when everything goes well with the birth. It did with Valegro's, and what a dear foal he was.

We called him Vainqueurfleur. 'Vainqueur' is French for victor, which was a good choice considering what he has gone on to achieve. He got on very well in the field, happily playing, and he got on very well with his mother.

We offer all our colt foals to Gertjan van Olst to buy. Valegro was born on a Saturday, and we called Gertjan on the Sunday to ask him if he would like a look at our new colt. On the Monday morning he came to our place, saw Valegro, and said he would have him. When Valegro was weaned, Gertjan bought him, and we followed his progress with Gertjan for the next few years.

After the stallion selection he was of course sold to Carl, and we heard about his first win, the Badminton Young Dressage Horse Championship, with Lucy Cartwright in 2006. Then we read in the KWPN magazine *In de Strengen* that he had won championships as a five- and six-year-old in England, and later read all about him coming second to Edward

Gal in Zwolle in 2011. The next time we saw Valegro was later in 2011 at Rotterdam with the team, and that was the first time we met Charlotte. It was lovely to meet her and Carl, and she seemed so happy to meet Valegro's breeders.

After that we had to see them as much as we could. We were there the following year when Valegro won everything in Rotterdam, and of course for the Olympic Games in London, then the Europeans in Herning and the World Cup qualifier in Amsterdam, and then of course Caen. So, we have been there for every championship, and it has been amazing to have been part of it. It is very special to see Valegro in Holland, his country of birth and our home, and we had a wonderful time at Amsterdam in 2015 and were so happy to meet up with Charlotte and Carl and the whole team from England. We are so very proud of what Valegro and Charlotte do at the very top of dressage sport.

One of the most unforgettable times was in 2014 at s'Hertogenbosch where Carl and Charlotte and Valegro did a clinic in front of a full stadium to celebrate Valegro winning the 2013 KWPN Horse of the Year title. It was unbelievable that this was our foal! Another was the year before when the World Breeding Federation for Sports Horses invited us to Doha, Qatar, to receive an award as the breeders of the most successful horse of the 2013 WBFSH Dressage ranking. Each of the three breeders – in dressage, jumping and eventing – received a very special prize, a Jaeger-LeCoultre Reverso watch, exclusively engraved with the WBFSH logo. The following year we were again invited, this time to Geneva, to receive the 2014 WBFSH prize. This time Jaeger-LeCoultre presented Maartje with a ladies' watch – she is becoming quite a 'watch woman'!

It is lovely that Valegro is Number One in the world. For us, he will always be Number One. We are so very proud of him. We are looking forward to seeing how his full sister gets on. She is only one year old. She is just like Valegro, in another colour, and her name is Jalegrofleur. Charlotte has already met her and liked her, but we won't sell her for now. We'd like to breed from her first. But for now, she is simply growing up in the field, just like her brother did.

Valegro as a foal with his dam, Maifleur.

Left: Father and son – Negro and Valegro with Gertjan van Olst and the Hanses at the KWP.N stallion selection in 's-Hertogenbosch, Netherlands, 2012, on the day when Negro was awarded his Preferent Predicate.

Below: Gertjan van Olst showing Valegro to the KWP.N stallion inspectors, 2005.

Bottom: Valegro looked amazing at the KWP.N inspection, but was not approved as a stallion. His was to be a different path.

3 A WINNING START

We had to cope with Valegro's head-shaking in the beginning, as Caroline Dawson, my head girl at the time, relates, and his big canter was a disadvantage in those early days, as it threw up the dust on his face, which he hated. Even so, he won the Shearwater four-year-old championship at the 2006 Nationals, but the best result that year was his Badminton Young Horse Championship with Lucy Cartwright up. Jan Brink, who had won European individual bronze with Björsells Briar at the Hickstead Europeans in 2003, among many other accolades, had come over from Sweden to judge and he loved the horse. It was very exciting for all of us, but especially for Lucy, who was Badminton-bred and so a hugely popular local winner.

It was around this time, when I was on the selection panel for the first rung of the World Class Performance programme, that I spotted a young rider who I thought had potential. I realised when I sat on her horse, Fernandez, how well trained he was and that he had grand prix potential. I talked to his rider afterwards and she bombarded me with questions. I thought she was worth keeping in touch with, but I had no room for another pupil until the following year. When she did come for a lesson, though, I liked her attitude and suggested she stay on for a few days to work as cover for a staff member who was on leave. That pupil was Charlotte Dujardin, and she's been here ever since.

Previous page: Carl riding four-year-old Valegro to claim the Shearwater Supreme Championship in 2006.

Above: Lucy Cartwright on Valegro: 'I adored everything about him.'

Left: Carl's annual training display at Badminton Horse Trials: Valegro with Lucy Cartwright up.

*The Hester team used to be based with Anne Seifert-Cohn, a few miles from Carl's current base in Gloucestershire. **Lucy Cartwright**, who came to work with Carl after finishing her GCSEs, and stayed for six years before setting up on her own nearby, was there when Valegro arrived.*

I thought Valegro was beautiful the moment I saw him. He always had such a wonderful character. Now he is so famous, it feels surreal that I ever had anything to do with him! I will never forget the first time I sat on Valegro, although I always think of him as Blueberry – 'Bluebs', I called him. He'd been backed, but was just starting out, so Carl was lungeing him with me up. Valegro's canter was so huge it felt as if I was going to be jumped off.

His first-ever outing was to a judges' seminar at FEI judge and rider Christian Landolt's. It was a good way of getting him out and about. Then his first competitive show was with me at Hunters Equestrian Centre, with Peter Storr judging. We only just kept the canter in the boards, but Bluebs was perfectly behaved, of course!

Winning the Badminton Young Horse final on Blueberry in 2006 when he was four was amazing. It is a bit of a blur, because I was so young and so excited to be judged by Jan Brink, an international rider and medallist for Sweden, as well as to be riding round with Carl on Uthopia. It certainly was what dreams are made of, yet Carl was just amazing and so supportive and genuinely happy for me, even though he and 'Uti' were second. He warmed me up on the grass between the lorries, and again Blueberry was just perfect and did not put a foot wrong throughout. My own horse had gone lame at the time, and Carl was so kind letting me ride Blueberry. I treated him as if he was my own and I adored everything about him; he was so friendly, and inquisitive as a baby.

Naturally I missed him when Charlotte started to ride him, but thank goodness she did, as I knew deep down I was too small (I'm just 5 foot 2 inches) and not experienced enough at the time. I groomed for Carl at the Badminton Young Horse final the following year when he won on Blueberry, which was really fun. It flooded that year and we couldn't get him home, so Carl had to warm up hacking around the estate lanes, and Bluebs ended up staying with my mum for a few days, as she lived just down the road from Badminton. And then to top it off, Carl also gave me the winner's cheque instead of the groom's – I remember sending him a text saying, 'I have the cheque and the horse – we're off!'

The day I left Carl's to set up on my own I held it together until the moment I said goodbye to Carl and Blueberry. Thinking of all this again reminds me what a bond we form with these animals. It makes me want to go back and work for Carl again!

Caroline Dawson *was Carl's head girl and travelling groom for many years. She then went to work for Anne and Gertjan van Olst in the Netherlands before returning briefly to Carl's yard, after which she became an equine veterinary nurse. She was with Carl at the van Olsts when Valegro returned from that fateful stallion show.*

We hadn't long been at the van Olsts' yard when Gertjan arrived back from the first round of a stallion selection with a lorryload of colts. Since I was busy settling Peanuts (Escapado) and whoever else we had with us into their stables, I didn't pay particular attention, but I always enjoyed watching Gertjan loose-school the youngsters – he has such empathy with them – so I went to watch. It's ironic that Blueberry was deemed too small to pass the first round of inspections, as since then he has grown into a machine! I remember thinking that he moved very well and had an extremely pretty head, but almost looked a bit 'cobby' in his body. Still, Carl liked him, and had him castrated and sent over to England.

Darren Mattia and I leant over him a few times in the stable, and then Blueberry was sent away to Sandra Biddlecombe to be backed. When he returned to Carl's yard, Lucy Cartwright took up the reins, but he hadn't been with us for long when he began to head-shake. We tried numerous herbal remedies, each one promising a cure, as well as nose nets and whatever else was trending at the time, but all to no avail. We weren't sure if sunlight or pollen was the trigger, and the problem seemed to escalate. At times he shook so violently that I was afraid, what with that and his enormous canter, little Lucy would be sent into orbit! In the stable and on the ground Bluebs had a temperament to die for, but the head-shaking was a problem until Carl worked out it was mainly caused by dust being kicked up, and a double bridle – which sits on an acupressure point – provided a solution.

But he was small – Carl thought too small – so Blueberry joined Carl, Peanuts and me on a journey back across the Channel when we were on our way to another international competition. Blueberry was dropped off at the van Olsts to be sold, and the rest of us went on to our party. Whilst we were at the show, the van Olsts put one of their work riders up on Blueberry and advised Carl he should keep him, even though they'd already had an offer for him. So we brought him home again. What we did learn from this trip was that he was a very good traveller!

Lucy continued to ride him with much determination. She gained numerous wins on him, the highlight being that Badminton Young Horse Championship in 2006. It was around this time that Charlotte joined the yard and began to ride him also. Since I was generally involved in the tacking up and washing off of horses between exercise, I didn't always see them working, but each time I saw Blueberry out it was obvious there was a bond developing between him and Charlotte. She always sported a huge grin when she was on his back. I'll never forget the first line of tempi changes she rode on him. I think Carl had her change every fifth or sixth stride, and her smile just grew and grew and grew as Blueberry produced a humungous clean change each time she asked. The pair of them looked thrilled, and it was so exciting that I walked away with a grin on my face too.

At the end of 2007, I left Carl and went to work for the van Olsts, where I cared for Negro, Blueberry's sire. I watched Blueberry develop from afar, and took pride in caring for Negro, who also has an impeccable character.

On my return to England, I went to work for Carl part-time. It was strange to go back after having been head girl, but I was privileged to hack Blueberry and give him a couple of light schooling sessions, under Carl's eye, after some time off. Even though we were just stretching and doing a few transitions I lapped up the incredible feel he gave me. I was very touched when Carl asked me if I would like to accompany him and Charlotte to Vidauban CDI. By this point I had begun working in an equine veterinary hospital and it was mid stud season, so I regretfully turned the offer down. I really wish I hadn't – but Alan went instead, and the rest is history.

It always gives me a warm feeling when people talk about Valegro without knowing that I used to work for Carl. I look at what he has achieved and cast my mind back to the little cobby pony who came off the lorry in Holland. I bet the KWPN are kicking themselves now!

Caroline Dawson with Escapado (known as Peanuts), Carl's former Olympic ride, who has now retired and lives with her near Carl's yard.

Charlotte was a strong rider when she came, and Valegro was a strong horse – strong in his body and inclined to be strong in his mouth – so I put them together. And as Charlotte had the chance to ride the more advanced horses, so her thirst for knowledge, her enthusiasm and her strong work ethic kept on impressing me and reminding me of myself at her age. Even then, while she and Valegro were learning and growing up together, she knew that she wanted to be an Olympic rider.

Collection is the crux of grand prix work, and some people (that's you, Stephen Clarke!) thought that huge canter of Valegro's would be difficult to collect. But his body is like a rubber ball, and Charlotte has a God-given talent for teaching a horse the collected movements. While she needed a lot of mentoring and guidance, as every young person does (even if they don't think they do), on how to pace the processes of training and working up to a competition, the beaming smiles when she achieved something new with Valegro came many and often.

Valegro won the novice national title with Charlotte in 2007, and both the elementary and medium championships in the following year. They won the 2009 winter advanced medium championship, but at the nationals that year Valegro was on early in the morning, so we didn't stick to the usual plan of riding him twice and as a result he was 'hot' in the test. It only took something clattering in the walkway and a moment's lost concentration to cost them the championship and leave them second. That was the only championship they didn't win!

In the following year, 2010, Valegro won the Prix St Georges National Championship, and that's when I first went on record as saying that the goal for Valegro and Charlotte was the London Olympics. Charlotte hadn't been happy with the test and came out grumbling, but I just let her take Valegro back to his stable as I turned to the Horse & Country TV camera and said that London 2012 was the aim.

Jan Brink (pictured above with Björsells Briar) has accumulated seven international championship medals – a record for a Swedish rider – with three different horses; Kleber Martini, Björsells Fontana and Björsells Briar, with whom he won silver at the Hickstead European Championships in 2003. After riding Briar at the World Cup Final in Las Vegas in 2009, he retired from international competition to concentrate on training horses and riders and running the stallion station he operates at his centre, Tullstorp Dressage, in southern Sweden, as well as spending more time with his wife Catharina. Valegro's sire Negro is one of the stallions Jan represents in Sweden.

It was a super opportunity to be invited to judge the Badminton Young Horse Championship in 2006. Catharina and I were invited by the Duke and Duchess of Beaufort to stay at Badminton House. We had a lovely dinner, and I was a little worried the following day that Carl was competing in the class as he had been at the dinner as well. We hadn't talked about the competition, but I didn't want anyone to think I'd be influenced!

I remember thinking that Valegro looked really athletic, although he was small, and he looked steady and easy-going for such a young horse. He was only four years old and was ridden by a slight girl, Lucy Cartwright, while Carl rode Uthopia in the five-year-old group, which he won, although I placed Valegro first in the championship. He was not the extreme 'flashy' type, but really steady in his gaits, in his rhythm. I really liked this particular young horse competition, but many, for me, are won by horses you never see at grand prix level. They may be big movers, but they are not quick enough in their action to be able to lengthen and shorten. Although Valegro was green and young, he could shorten his stride and was steady in his frame, and you could already see that this horse could be useful.

It is amazing how things develop, as it was not until three years ago that someone told me Valegro was the horse I had judged in that class. But when you see him now, he makes everything look extremely easy; there is so much power but no pushing or pulling, there is huge movement but no change in rhythm. I could see that back then. And what is so good is that this is what everyone is looking for now in dressage: harmony as well as expression. It was good to see Valegro back then and it is great to see him now.

Above: A winner at just four years old!

Right: Carl rode Valegro to win that Shearwater Supreme Championship in 2006.

Far right: The look of a professor – even at such a tender age. Valegro won the four-year-old title before his win in the Supreme Championship.

Four times an Olympian (including at London 2012), **Richard Davison** (pictured above) is a long-time friend, team-mate and adviser to Carl. An international trainer and former British dressage team captain, Richard completed his term of office as the British World Class Performance Manager, a post he held for four years, masterminding the strategic plan behind Britain's most successful period of international successes.

I recall judging Valegro in the final Young Horse Championship at the British National Championships; I don't remember whether he was in the four- or five-year-old section. He was always full of energy, sometimes more than he could contain in those early years, but when he came to performing the canter section I did not hesitate to award him a ten. I can picture it now; that canter had everything you could ever want in a canter. I wonder if that was the first ten of his career?

Above: Charlotte and Valegro take the 2008 Medium Championship at Stoneleigh…

Top right: … and the Shearwater Supreme Championship completes the haul. Jeremy Lawton of Shearwater Insurance presents the prize.

Right: Valegro won the Elementary Open Championship as well that year.

Far right: Valegro calmly surveying the crowd, seeming to say, 'Thank you – glad you enjoyed it!'

Francis Verbeek (pictured below) is a trainer, clinician and FEI 5* International Dressage judge from the Netherlands who has officiated at many championships, including the 2014 World Equestrian Games and the 2015 World Cup Final.

I saw Valegro for the first time when he was five or six years old. I was judging at an auction in Great Britain with Carl Hester, and he had just brought Valegro along to train the horse. When I watched, I was really impressed with the quality of the basic gaits and the balance and expression the horse already had at that age.

Later on I was lucky enough to judge the 'super horse' Valegro at many big championships. I have the feeling that he always gets better and better.

Valegro is amazing. Everyone who sees him will remember him for ever as almost the perfect horse.

2010: Valegro and Charlotte are
National Small Tour Champions.

That huge canter in evidence at the prize-giving (left)…

… and in the tests (above).

4 THE ROAD TO LONDON

In 2010 Valegro had made his international debut in Spain on what's known as the 'Sunshine Tour' with a perfect winning record at Prix St Georges and just one second place at Intermediaire I, so of course he stole the show. We've never competed any of the horses heavily, and being able to keep Valegro at home and in training until the National Championships gave us just time to get the longer-term game plan under way.

The plan started at our next international in January 2011, in the much colder setting of Zwolle in Holland, where I was riding Charlotte's horse Fernandez (or Dez) for his first grand prix, and it was the ideal opportunity for Charlotte to start Valegro indoors at small tour level. He didn't win the Prix St Georges, instead coming second to Edward Gal on Voice, but the buzz about him started. He was definitely getting noticed. Wim Ernes, who later became the Dutch team coach and then chairman of the KWPN Stallion Licensing Committee, but who was already very well known as an international judge, came up and told me Valegro was one of the best young horses he had ever seen at that level.

While the priority was to get Dez and my horse Uthopia (Uti) qualified, Valegro was waiting in the wings for his grand prix debut. I had been working with Charlotte for a whole month preparing them for it. Valegro was so intelligent that there was no need to try the exercises many other horses benefit from, such as getting him not to anticipate. Unusually, the plan was just to teach him to do the test. It's rare to do only the test movements with a horse, but that was Valegro's way – show him the route, and he'll take it. Of course he was very green and there was still not enough time for him to know exactly where he was going in the test, but at Addington, on his grand prix debut, he zapped the class with nearly 75 per cent and scored his first of many tens.

Previous page: Rotterdam 2011: Charlotte and Valegro follow chef d'équipe Dickie Waygood to the arena for their freestyle test. On their team debut, the team won gold, but it was Carl and Uthopia's year in the individual with two silvers.

Above: 2011 started at Zwolle for Valegro.

Right: He may not have won, but Valegro was being talked about.

Wim Ernes (pictured above) is the national coach for the Dutch dressage team. To take this post he had to stand down from his FEI official judging role, during which he judged at many internationals and championships. He has also been very involved with the KWPN, and stands down as President of the Licensing Committee at the end of 2015.

I clearly remember in Zwolle in January 2011 when I saw this horse competing in a small tour competition. I hadn't seen him before, and he didn't win, but it struck me that this was a very interesting horse for the future. I saw him for the second time a few months later at Vidauban. I gave Valegro his first ten for extended trot and I remember saying to the show manager, 'If you are issuing a press release, it would be wise to say that we have probably seen the gold medal winner of the future.' Just a year later, as I came out of my judging box at the London Olympics, I received a text from the show manager at Vidauban. It simply said, 'You were right.'

To have been present at these two remarkable cornerstones in Valegro's life is great, as it is to watch him.

Judy Harvey *is an international rider, television commentator and FEI dressage judge, and was Charlotte's first dressage trainer.*

Even when Valegro was a young horse, it was very obvious that he knew he was pretty good. I watched his first grand prix at Addington. It wasn't an international, or a premier league, just a winter show in the evening, and he did a fantastic test. It was Charlotte's first grand prix as well, and as Valegro came into the first piaffe he stopped – he didn't know what to do. Charlotte nudged him with her legs, and he just went into the most brilliant piaffe. I was already jealous at this point! Well, they scored 75 per cent and won the class. Carl was in the warm-up area as the score was announced and was on the phone in seconds. I thought he was trying to sell the horse (which it turns out he wasn't), so I went over to him and said, 'If you sell that effing horse, I'll never speak to you again.' Thank goodness he hadn't been going to sell him. Anyway, Valegro stayed and he isn't going anywhere.

My horse was stabled next to Valegro at Hagen when Valegro broke the world record for grand prix special. He is a true professional, but seeing him in the stable he could be any horse, standing calmly and looking around with interest at the goings-on with just a rope across his door. Then this regular guy goes out and breaks records!

Being able to commentate for the BBC on those tests at Greenwich during the London Olympics in 2012 was amazing. Seeing Charlotte and Valegro go on from the start to claim gold medals was unforgettable – I was on tenterhooks in the commentary box. I have been on a few judges' courses since then, and Valegro is now referred to as the example of how dressage should be. It's a huge tribute to Carl's training. He's done such a great job. Of course Charlotte had the temperament and the competitive instinct, but it needed Carl's steadying hand and maturity to make it happen.

Above: Charlotte on Valegro, Carl on Uthopia.

Left: Judy Harvey (at right) with Charlotte Dujardin.

Top right: With Alan Davies – another true partnership in Valegro's life.

Vidauban, in the south of France, just north of St Tropez, was the next port of call in March 2011, and it would be the venue for Valegro's first-ever international grand prix. Thinking of the Sunshine Tour, my rationale was that Vidauban would still be warm, but the journey to get there would be a lot shorter. I was right on the second count and very wrong on the first. It poured! But Charlotte was determined to get her qualifying score on Valegro, and that swung the decision to start rather than withdraw. And what a debut it was. Valegro won both his grands prix, and both specials. That is a phenomenal international debut for anyone, but for a green horse to do virtually mistake-free tests, albeit without the polish of a seasoned competitor, was astonishing.

Vidauban was also the first trip with Alan Davies as groom. I'd known Alan for years, and I asked if he'd come with us this time as Caroline was leaving to start her new career as a veterinary nurse. Of course Alan has never left, and he's been by Valegro's side ever since.

As I was campaigning Uthopia, bringing him back to the arena after some time off, as well as bringing Charlotte and Valegro on, it was becoming pretty clear that these two horses would be forces to be reckoned with. At the end of April, we headed back to France, to Saumur, where Uti had won the year before, and he won again with 74 per cent. Valegro, at nine a year younger than Uti, was just 1 per cent behind in second place – and then he and Charlotte beat me and Uti by a sniff to win the grand prix special! My plan looked as if it was on track.

*Belgian-born **Robrecht ('Rob') Cnockaert** studied veterinary medicine at Ghent University. His equine consultancy practice specialises in the care of performance horses. Robrecht and Carl met at the Rotterdam Nations Cup show in 2008, and Rob has enjoyed contributing to the veterinary care of Carl's horses ever since. Rob lives in Nottinghamshire with his wife Jennifer, their two children and an ever-expanding menagerie.*

I have known Blueberry since he was quite a young horse. I would love to say that from the moment I met him I was aware (as Carl and Charlotte seemed to be) of the greatness for which he was destined, but in fact he simply struck me as a very sweet, laid-back character. Little did I know the vast range of emotions through which this unassuming, generous little horse would take me in the years to come.

When I think of Valegro, it is not his overwhelming talent and power which first come to mind – it is his honesty, integrity and kindness. He is a horse with a work ethic; giving 100 per cent of himself every time, everywhere, in everything he does – and making it look easy while doing it! I would love to know what he is thinking as he peers out at the crowds during yet another prize-giving. There is a wisdom in his expression, accompanied by a sparkle of humour in his eyes, perhaps amused by his own private joke.

It is a humbling experience to be privy to some of the more private and touching moments behind the scenes. Watching the fierce loyalty with which his groom Alan cares for him is innately reassuring, because a horse that gives so generously of himself and inspires the love of so many deserves nothing less. One thing is certain: Valegro is loved and adored by an entire team of people who constantly dedicate themselves to his care – what an honour it is to be part of such a team. To say that the process has also aged me considerably would be an understatement! And yet I would not have had it any other way.

Valegro's huge heart, astounding talent and extraordinary disposition make it easy to understand how he has captured the hearts of a nation. He has most certainly captured mine.

Right: Valegro was proving to be one cool horse. Carl and Charlotte hug while Dickie Waygood beams.

Far right: Valegro and Charlotte training for their team debut at Rotterdam 2011; with (behind) Laura Bechtolsheimer (now Tomlinson) and Mistral Hojris.

Below: Valegro tries to eat Robrecht Cnockaert's Olympic accreditation, London 2012.

At the beginning, the conscious plan was to get these two horses, Uti and Blueberry (as we call Uthopia and Valegro at home), to the Europeans with Charlotte's Fernandez as a spare (Dez was sold after the Europeans to Norway's Catherine Rasmussen, as by then it was clear Valegro was to be Charlotte's No. 1), and to build up to achieving big scores. It was a big ask, especially for a young and inexperienced combination like Charlotte and Valegro, but it was obvious from early on that confidence was not going to be an issue. Charlotte's competitive streak was always strong, but the more shows she did, the more she rose to the challenge, and Valegro – well, he was proving to be one cool horse.

We were well supported by the GB team management and selectors, but I don't think anyone really foresaw at that stage how amazing the two horses would be in 2011, or what was to come from Valegro. It was to be Uthopia's year, really, but with scores in the mid to high seventies for a combination very, very new to grand prix, it was obvious that Valegro, at a year younger than Uti, was going to make headlines in the future.

Richard Davison, *the international trainer and leading British dressage rider, has known Valegro for many years.*

As soon as Valegro started learning the grand prix exercises, it was pretty clear that it was easy for him. Whenever I called in to Carl's yard over the years, Carl was more and more excited about him, and I remember him calling me over when Valegro was only seven years old and asking Charlotte to show me how easily he was learning his one-time changes. Then, during Valegro's first international grand prix in Vidauban, Carl sent me a text telling me he was the most natural grand prix horse he'd ever had. But I suspect even Carl didn't realise exactly how special Valegro was, what he would go on to win, or the world records he would achieve.

To make your team debut and go home with a medal is the stuff dreams are made of, but it was a dream come true for Charlotte and Valegro in Rotterdam's Kralingse Bos park at the European Championships in August 2011. Uthopia won the grand prix, which Valegro and Charlotte would go on to do at the London Olympics the following year. Adelinde Cornelissen was second for the Dutch home team, followed by Germany's Matthias Rath on the controversial 'wonder horse' Totilas, and then in fourth place were Charlotte and Valegro with a whopping 78 per cent, with Laura Bechtolsheimer and Mistral Hojris just 1 per cent behind. It was an all-time record team score, and despite Holland taking the bronze behind Germany, it was incredible how much the Dutch spectators took our two Dutch-bred horses to their hearts. Those minutes watching Valegro and Charlotte do their grand prix were the most nerve-racking of my entire life, and I sobbed all the way through. Jon Stroud's photographs of me hiding behind a pillar as I watched Valegro's beautiful test recorded every moment. All the training, all the planning, all the work, all the pressure – everything paid off. But then things started to go a little bit awry.

The most nerve-racking moments of Carl's life, watching Valegro and Charlotte's grand prix in Rotterdam 2011.

Fourth in the grand prix, contributing to team gold with a record score in Rotterdam 2011.

Right: Sooner or later they'd have to cope on their own. Valegro and Charlotte in Rotterdam.

Below: Team gold on their team debut for Valegro and Charlotte – incredible for all!

We knew that sooner or later we'd be drawn to ride close to each other, but for Valegro and Charlotte to have to cope on their own without me just six months into their grand prix career was a big ask. As I concentrated on Uti, who won silver in the special and the freestyle, Valegro's tests had some lovely highlights but lots of mistakes as Charlotte lost concentration, and she went wrong in her freestyle too. It was unlike her, but perfectly understandable at her first major team competition, and it was all part of a huge learning curve. It was fabulous that my medal haul included those individual medals – my first ones – but the main aim was for Valegro and Charlotte to come home with team gold too, and our triumph was an incredible feeling for all of us.

Stephen Clarke *(pictured above with Valegro) is the FEI Judge General, a former international rider and trainer, and the most senior and respected dressage judge in the world.*

It's funny – I remember being wildly impressed by Valegro in a young horse class but saying to Carl, 'Good luck collecting that canter.' I suspect he thought 'bloody Stephen Clarke' for a while after that. Of course the horse has been trained brilliantly, but physically he is so naturally strong in his hindquarters and able to carry weight that everything looks effortless. He is the only horse in the world that has everything as a highlight – there are no weaknesses. It's freakish, really.

The London Olympics were like a fairy story when Valegro and Charlotte won two golds having done so few grands prix. I thought then it would be interesting to see what happens, but I am totally in awe of how Charlotte and Valegro cope with the pressure and keep turning out brilliant tests. That's what has impressed me most.

Judging Valegro at the World Cup Final in Las Vegas in 2015 was a pleasure, of course, but what brought a tear to the eye – and you could see many in the crowd brushing tears away – was how Valegro came in for the prize-giving and stood four-square in that crazy place, with the reins slack on his neck and the sweetest expression on his face. That said it all, really. That horse is the whole package, mentally and physically.

Valegro's next outing was to Olympia in December. The show has an amazing Christmas spirit and atmosphere, and it is always great to ride in front of such an enthusiastic crowd. It can spook a lot of horses and can certainly make them 'hot', but Valegro kept his cool. When he and Charlotte won the grand prix, it marked a brilliant end to his first year at this level – they were the only combination to break the 80 per cent barrier with 81; a personal best, obviously. The freestyle result could hardly have been closer, with the first three – Laura and Mistral Hojris, Charlotte and Valegro, and me with Uti – all on fractionally different 83 per cent scores, and Laura became the first British rider ever to win the Olympia World Cup qualifier. Valegro's huge trot extensions and wonderful piaffe were highlights, and Charlotte was very happy with him. He was hotter than in the grand prix, and was a bit tense to begin with, so the halt at the start didn't happen and they also had mistakes in the tempi changes, but Charlotte salvaged that by repeating them, which was canny for only her second grand prix freestyle. For Valegro, at only nine the youngest horse in the class, to put up a performance like that in such an atmosphere was incredible, and Stephen Clarke, who was the President of the Ground Jury, called the result 'A dream come true from a national point of view.'

Valegro on his way to second place in the Olympia FEI World Cup qualifier. With Laura and Alf in first and Carl and Uti in third, it was a British line-up, all on 83 per cent scores.

Early in 2012, the Olympic year, the organisers of the World Dressage Masters invited Charlotte and me to compete in Florida. Being such a long trip, it wasn't one for Uti, so instead I took Wie Atlantico who'd been offered by his owner/rider Fiona Bigwood as she was pregnant at the time, but since Valegro was already proving himself to be a good traveller I thought it would be a good show for him and it would be an opportunity to introduce him to the USA. Both horses travelled beautifully, which was a huge relief.

Valegro and Charlotte were second to Steffen Peters and Ravel, the US home favourites, in a very close match, but this was another big atmosphere and Valegro was hot. He made a couple of big mistakes, but it was lovely to see the American audience so thrilled to see him, as they'd heard he was one of our up-and-coming stars.

In the freestyle, where Atlantico and I finished fourth, it was another duel between Valegro and Ravel. In this sport, results can be significantly affected by one judge's marks and it is something every dressage rider simply has to learn to live with, otherwise it would drive us all crazy. That is exactly what happened here, when one judge placed Steffen on a big score and Charlotte under 80 per cent, although the overall difference was fractional. Steffen actually thought Charlotte had won and very graciously congratulated her! But more importantly, the trip showed Valegro was growing in experience and had come on a stage since Olympia. In the grand prix prize-giving, however, he did something very unusual. There was a heart-stopping moment when he reared and stood bolt upright, nearly vertical. He had never done it before and has never done it since.

Above: Valegro's introduction to the USA. Warming up for the World Dressage Masters, Florida 2012.

Right: A shock for Charlotte in the Florida prize-giving as Valegro stands bolt upright – the only time he has done so.

*Former Olympic rider and List 1 judge **Patricia ('Trish') Gardiner** FBHS (pictured above) competed at grand prix level for over 25 years and was a regular member of the British dressage team between 1977 and 1991, when she was on the team for the European Championships with Carl and the Bechtolsheimers' Rubelit von Unkenruf. She represented Great Britain at the Seoul Olympics in 1988 with her Thoroughbred Wily Imp, and later competed another lovely Thoroughbred, Moon Tiger.*

I love hacking Valegro out twice a week, and feel very privileged that Carl allows me the opportunity. I don't own a horse any more, so it's a great joy to sit on a proper dressage horse and feel the strength and the power and the wonderful training, even though I am only hacking out. Actually Carl did let me ride him in the arena one time, and everything felt amazing there too. I was very pleased I could still press all the right buttons!

Valegro is a charming individual with perfect manners while being ridden, but, like most fit horses, he can be a bit grumpy when being tacked up. He's very enthusiastic and walks at a terrific rate, which makes hacking out rather unsociable, as nobody can keep up. He's very brave and always gives a lead to the young horses past all the scary things one meets around the roads.

He loves to snatch at the leaves in the hedgerows, as food is a very important feature of his life, but his manners are perfect and he has a very endearing personality, so everybody loves him to bits, including me.

Back home again, it was all about fine-tuning and consistency, ironing out any potential creases, and working out the programme to bring Valegro up to fitness for each show in the build-up to the London 2012 Olympics, whilst still letting him have some down-time and relaxation; hacking and his much-loved time in the field. Both Uti and Blueberry were well known by now, and they no longer needed to be got used to travelling or acclimatising to different surroundings, so we could keep shows to a minimum, but the first big outdoor show of the season, Horses and Dreams, in Hagen, near Osnabrück in Germany, was a must. Not least as the show always has a country theme, and in April 2012, with the Olympics coming up, not surprisingly it was 'Horses and Dreams meets Great Britain'.

*Training at home – Valegro trains in the
school four times a week. He has plenty
of breaks and time for a nose-scratch!*

And then of course there's the all-important hacking with Alan or Trish: Trish (pictured here) takes him out on Wednesdays.

Horses and Dreams was where Valegro would meet many of the medal challengers, and where he and Charlotte could contest the grand prix special – which was important, as it would count towards the team result at the Olympics. And what a result it was! Valegro and Charlotte won the grand prix on 81 per cent, then scored 88 per cent to set a new world record for the special. This was their first world record score, beating the previous record set by Edward Gal and Totilas by nearly 2 per cent. It was a flawless performance, flowing and amazing to watch. Almost as amazingly, I was hugely calm watching! At the end, the commentator called for a standing ovation and the huge crowd responded. Charlotte had to bite her lip in the prize-giving as her tears welled. She knew she had ridden a good test, but she couldn't see the scoreboard, so she didn't know the result until I told her. All she could say was, 'Oh my God.'

Above: The team on the way to the arena in Hagen, and Carl gives Charlotte some last words of encouragement.

Right: Alan takes charge of Valegro for the prize-giving – Charlotte's overwhelmed.

Horses and Dreams also helped us when the soundtrack there gave us the idea for the music for Valegro's new freestyle, the Big Ben programme designed by Tom Hunt. Charlotte and Valegro would première the new routine and music at Hartpury, our local show venue in Gloucestershire and the final outing before the Olympics in August. I decided not to take Uti so that I could be there 100 per cent for Charlotte and Valegro. There was a mere two weeks between Hartpury and the Olympics, and I wanted Charlotte to have full confidence to go to London and pull in a huge score with Valegro. Even in that special at Hagen, we could see that there was more to come: Valegro still had more to give.

*Top: The first world record – Hagen
2012 Grand Prix Special.*

*Above: Charlotte had to bite her lip – and
so did the trainer!*

Right: Valegro appreciates the carrots.

Maribel Alonso *was appointed to the FEI Dressage committee in 2014 and is a 5* FEI dressage judge. As well as judging and serving as a technical delegate at top shows around the world, including the Olympics and other major championship, Maribel has actively promoted the development of dressage throughout the Americas, spearheading the efforts of the Pan Am Games to raise the level of competition in order to qualify teams for the Olympics. Highly respected and much loved, she is also renowned for her fashion sense!*

I first saw Valegro and Charlotte on the 2010 Sunshine Tour, the season before they moved on to grand prix. I had no idea who they were. For me, this was just another British combination, one of the many we saw starting in the south of Spain in those days.

I did not judge the class that day, but as I was not working I watched the Prix St Georges. Valegro won, and although they didn't win the Intermediaire I because the performance was not as smooth, this was irrelevant compared with the emotion this horse made me feel.

I cannot find the words to describe it; that mixture of power and grace, harmony and lightness, elasticity and softness. It was simply beautiful.

Watching this super-powerful horse being ridden by a slim and elegant, young but not so tall rider, and being aware of this horse's power and his young age, I was amazed. He behaved like a true gentleman.

The never-ending dialogue, communion and bond that I perceived between horse and rider has always struck me, and it does not cease to impress me to this day.

Many words have been used to describe Valegro's incredible physical talents, but his mind and heart are the size of the world. I always have the feeling that he has chosen to give it all to Charlotte. She is without any doubt a gifted rider and has the ability to be a great leader. If we add to this equation the amazing talent of an outstanding trainer like Carl Hester, we get performances like the ones this combination delivers time after time.

Between them, Carl and Charlotte are writing a special chapter in the history of dressage.

For me, this is a trio that was made in heaven.

Above: Maribel Alons

Right: The dream team of Ca
Charlotte and Valegro – history make

Winnie Murphy *is the marketing manager at British Dressage (BD). She deals with all journalists' enquiries, keeps local and national press up to date about BD news and generally promotes the sport. She writes and updates rider biographies for international shows, is in charge of the BD trade stand, the members' marquee, banners and so on, and places advertising in the national press for key events as well as being involved with* British Dressage *magazine and the BD website. And of course, she is the 'go to' lady for the media where Valegro and Charlotte are concerned, so she's kept pretty busy.*

On my first day at BD, in March 2011, I was called in to Will Connell's office. Charlotte and Valegro had been to their first international big tour CDI in Vidauban, where they swept the board. Will said to play it down, people were getting unduly excited about the pairing, and it was still very early days for them to prove themselves. Quite right, I thought! I can laugh about it now: little did we know what was to come!

Sometimes I wish Valegro could actually talk and do the interviews himself – I'm sure at times Charlotte wishes that, too! He'd be a fascinating interviewee: eloquent, polished, giving quotes to die for and a story worthy of a Hollywood blockbuster, but at the same time understated and in no way bullish. I can just see him perched on Clare Balding's sofa, chatting away. The media love him – and Charlotte too. Small town girl from humble beginnings meets 'failed' bargain horse, and the partnership of a lifetime begins... (I wonder if Mr Spielberg is reading this?) He's introduced the media to the wonders of dressage, and they can't help but be captivated.

As an equine athlete, Valegro has revolutionised dressage. His manner, way of going, presence, attitude to work and powerful ease have never been matched, and probably never will be. We all said that previously in the days of Totilas, but Valegro is the full package – he ticks all the boxes, meets all the criteria and has the scales of training nailed. While he is truly outstanding, it is nonetheless a team effort, and I firmly believe that through Carl and Charlotte's training, management and dedication, Valegro has realised his potential – with a bit more still to come, I'm sure. For some years, the equestrian world has lacked equine pin-ups, and few horses have warranted a place on teenage walls since the days of Milton, Desert Orchid and Murphy Himself (am I showing my age?), but now Valegro adorns many walls up and down the country. Similarly, dressage has rarely seen young girls practising for hours in a bid to be the next Charlotte and Valegro, urging their little 'Welshies' to dance like their idols. Valegro and Charlotte have raised dressage to a new platform – they've put their own stamp on a very traditional sport with their flair, ease and natural ability, and they've somehow made it all very modern and captivated a new audience. Carl labelled Valegro 'The Professor', which is very apt as it sums up his ability, knowledge and command of dressage, but perhaps he should be 'the revolutionary' as well, as he has transformed our sport.

I've been privileged to look behind the scenes and see what Valegro is really like, and the wonderful thing is that he's every bit as special as you want him to be. Kind, gentle, a little bit cheeky, but with an aura of 'spectacular' about him. His unusual head with wide-set eyes, shapely cheekbones and narrow muzzle are distinctive, but you can't help look at him and smile – and feel like he's smiling right back at you.

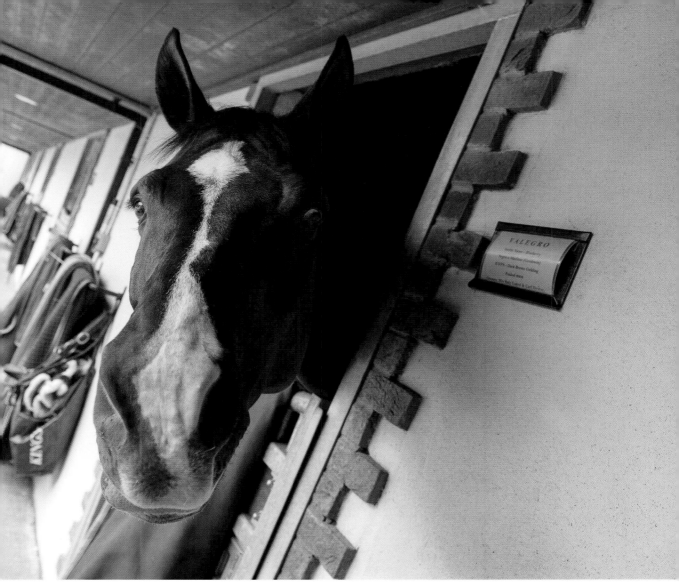

Above: Up for an interview, Valegro?

Left: For this TV crew, Alan gives the interview – one of many.

Far left: Winnie Murphy.

*Getting Valegro to shows all around the world takes a huge amount of organisation and administration, and that has been the domain of Carl's personal assistant, **Claudine Bichard**, throughout Valegro's career. Claudine has been organising Carl's and his horses' lives since 2000, and she combines the job with riding her own horse and looking after her family.*

At the beginning of each year Valegro's passport is checked to make sure it is up to date. To enable him to compete, he has to be registered with the FEI, and his British Dressage (BD) membership is renewed.

Also at the beginning of the year Carl will go through his competition plan for the next ten to twelve months, which I then submit to BD. An entry needs to be made for each international show on the plan. As soon as the show schedule has been released, a nominated entry is made via BD, stating all the requirements for each show – Valegro's arrival and departure dates, his passport number, the owners' details and any special requests. Carl now asks for a double stable!

Once the initial entry has been made, it is entered onto the FEI database and then confirmed. Next the travel needs to be organised. National and European shows are generally quite straightforward – it is just a case of booking a crossing to Europe for Blueberry, Alan and the lorry. The crossings and health papers are arranged via Lydia Boult, our agent at the Equine Logistics Company. Alan and Blueberry prefer to travel through the Eurotunnel now, just in case of rough weather at the ports.

Before setting off, and depending on where he is travelling to, Blueberry has to have a visit from vet Tim Beauregard, who completes his travel papers and checks that all his details are in order. A health certificate is applied for through Defra (the Department for Environment, Food and Rural Affairs) and, as well as this, he needs an export licence to allow him to leave and return to the UK.

When Blueberry returns from competition, all the paperwork is collected, and the export licence is kept for six months, as Defra can inspect it during that time to check it is in order. All the travel receipts are collected together, and because all athletes on the World Class Performance Plan receive some funding towards their travel and competition costs, some of these expenses can be claimed back.

On top of all this, there are sponsors to liaise with, dates to arrange for visits from Blueberry's fans, charity events to organise, and the odd lunch to cook as well!

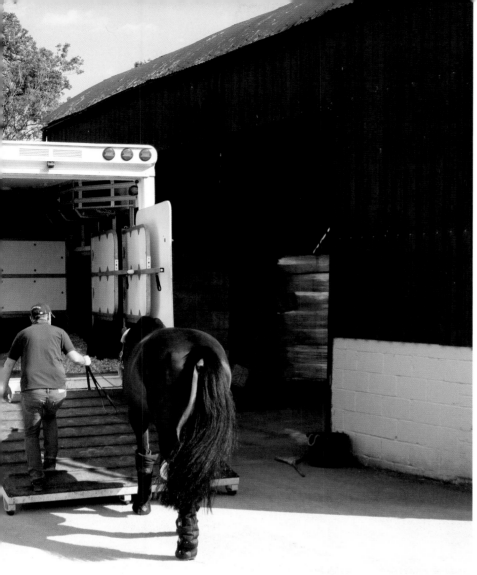

Left and below: On the road, whether it's long-distance in the big lorry or just a local trip, Alan ensures Valegro gets to his destination in the best possible shape.

Bottom left: Claudine Bichard and Carl checking travel details.

Valegro is known as Blueberry at home. And yes, that's a bit of bling on his bridle.

5 GIVING HIS ALL

After all the preparation, that August we were finally at the Olympics. This was what all our work had been leading towards, on our home turf in London – not just getting to Greenwich, but winning medals too. So the knowledge that Valegro and Charlotte had the chance of individual gold was exciting but also nerve-racking.

They went last for Team GB after Uti and I had landed 77.72 per cent on the first day and Laura and Mistral Hojris (Alf) got 76.83. Both Charlotte and Valegro were calm, but I wasn't, or not until they trotted into the arena to applause from the crowd. As Valegro showed off his paces and Charlotte just guided him, I watched, and my heart swelled with pride. They set a new Olympic grand prix record of 83.784 per cent. Charlotte had come to London with the innocence of a new Olympian, and here she was now, lapping up the whole thing and enjoying it.

There were no medals yet, as the team competition wouldn't be decided until after the special, and during our 'break' the Team GB showjumpers won gold, which upped the pressure on us. When the time came, I rode for all I could get on Uthopia, Laura upped her score with Alf by 2 per cent, and then it was once again up to Charlotte and Valegro. Sure enough, that amazing horse gave his all and clinched the gold, winning the first Olympic medal ever for a British dressage team. As the final rider's score was announced, history was made and the crowd went wild. Of course the atmosphere was incredible. I never thought I'd walk into an arena surrounded by a crowd waving Union flags and cheering – the wall of noise was amazing – but it did happen, and it was Valegro who made it happen.

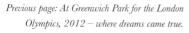

Previous page: At Greenwich Park for the London Olympics, 2012 – where dreams came true.

Above: As always, Alan is by the side of Valegro and Charlotte.

Right: Every championship starts with the vet check or 'trot up'.

Below: Appreciation from Team GBR including (in the red hat) HRH The Princess Royal.

Fiona Lawrence (pictured above) is the stable manager at Carl's Gloucestershire yard.

One of the things that stands out, I think, about 'Bluebs' is that he is still down to earth, although he does know how to work a camera! I have strong first memories of him as he was the first horse I rode when I came to Carl's. I remember thinking how lovely it was that he really enjoyed his work – he was very happy looking over hedges and up people's drives.

The first show I took him to was his elementary and medium regionals at Somerford Park in Cheshire in 2008. He really enjoyed his time in the arena, and I think he knew even then he was special. He won them both.

He also loves his food as much as his work. Even though he has his own hay net hanging up, he always tries to take mouthfuls from the other horses' nets as they're carried past his stable.

When you walk him in hand on the drive, and if it's the season when there are apples on the ground, if he can't reach one he will kick it until he can. It's really funny to watch. And also, if there are any leaves on the drive, he is like a hoover: they just disappear without his mouth moving.

It was a real privilege to be his groom at all his shows until he started grand prix, and of course at the Rotterdam Europeans and the Olympics.

We had a day off in Greenwich before the freestyle to music, the individual final, on the Thursday. I took Uti for a spin up the gallops, which had been put in for the eventers, before Charlotte and I had a practice session with Valegro. The facilities at Greenwich were superb, and the stables were set up so that Team GB had their horses in their own barn (and not too close to the loudspeakers either, which was good). The horses settled really well, and Alan and our yard manager Fiona Lawrence found it easy to get them to relax as long as they had their food – especially Valegro. There were fans installed in the stables, so they never got too warm, and the grooms also used a magnetic rug to warm up the horses' muscles before work and to relax them afterwards.

Charlotte had only ridden the final choreography of Valegro's new freestyle test once before, so of course felt a little short of practice. It was essential to go for a high degree of difficulty to win medals, but we were still debating whether to put in the planned piaffe pirouette at the end. As it turned out, it was to be the only movement Charlotte fluffed! Valegro was still aged only ten, and movements like this were going to be new to him. We knew at the start that he likes to know where he is going and he likes to know the programme (which of course he did for the grand prix and the special), but we were pleased with the practice and decided to go for it.

Gold! Valegro shows that amazing trot.

Jennie Loriston-Clarke MBE, FBHS blazed a trail for British dressage for many years, winning Britain's first World Championship medal (bronze), on Dutch Courage at Goodwood in 1978. She represented Great Britain at four Olympics, and was on the team at the World Equestrian Games in Stockholm in 1990 when Carl made his team debut. Jennie is an FEI judge for both dressage and eventing, and since retiring from international competition in 1995 has devoted her time to training horses and riders, judging, stewarding and, with her husband Anthony, running their breeding operation at Catherston Stud. She was previously chair of British Dressage and is now its president. She was the FEI steward at the London 2012 Olympics.

I first saw Valegro as a four-year-old at the National Championships, and thought how much presence he had for a gelding. He had impressive power, but did look strong! Always forward, ears pricked, he was completely on his rider's side, just like Dutch Courage and Dutch Gold, although so much better, and those are the ones that make it.

Despite all the hype, Valegro is so calm, especially after his tests, as if he is feeling satisfied with how it all went. At the Olympics he looked amazing. It was fascinating to see him at Aachen, with those mistakes, and the crowd gasping: I think these horses do feel disquieted when they sense something has gone wrong, and they obviously want to get it right. It was very difficult for Charlotte, but one has to remember they were still an awful lot better than many others!

Charlotte and Valegro have an amazing relationship. I have often thought how very generous it was of Carl not to take the ride himself. I am sure he would have ridden Valegro brilliantly, although he might have looked a bit tall. So Charlotte is a very lucky girl.

I have never judged Valegro, and doubt I ever will now, but I was stewarding at the Olympics when the freestyle result was announced. Well, I just couldn't believe it! Who would have thought twenty years ago that we'd be wiping the Germans' faces? The very interesting thing as a steward is watching the different training methods; some nations who shall remain nameless work their horses so hard, but the Brits are such a pleasure to watch. That's so good to see, and I hope Valegro's relatives – especially U-Genius as a stallion – will prove a real advertisement for British breeding too.

The individual test, the freestyle, was the last equestrian competition at the Olympics, so while the crowd in the stadium was the biggest and noisiest ever, the stables and the backstage atmosphere were quite eerie – quiet and empty.

I'd already done what I had set out to do, and I had that team gold to take home, so Uti and I just went out to enjoy ourselves without medal pressure, and then I hopped off and went out to watch Charlotte and Valegro. Adelinde Cornelissen and Parzival for the Netherlands had achieved the huge score of 88 per cent, so my thought was that Valegro had to be foot-perfect to beat that. He wasn't. There was a miscommunication in that last piaffe pirouette – it was nothing really, but was it everything where the gold was concerned? We were philosophical and fairly calm; there wasn't any disappointment involved – but then someone leant over from the stands and screamed, 'You've done it!' and the crowd went berserk. Charlotte just sobbed. Everyone did, actually!

Right: Jennie Loriston-Clarke.

Total concentration from Charlotte and Valegro.

All of us who know Valegro could see he had given every last bit of effort, and now he was tired. It was another half an hour or so until the prize-giving, and then just the top three went in: Valegro, Parzival and Alf, who'd won bronze with Laura. The crowd had done a Mexican wave just before the horses came in, and the atmosphere was electric. Valegro stood rock-solid amid that euphoria. Fiona and Alan managed to keep him so still by Fiona putting some sugar lumps between her fingers and getting him to lick them slowly while Alan scratched his neck. So Valegro was a perfect gentleman while the ceremony was going on.

Back home again afterwards, it was back to grass and hacking, light times for the horses who had achieved what a few years before would have been thought unachievable by British riders, and of course Valegro was now a household name.

For those who hadn't got to the Olympics, giving them an opportunity to see Valegro and concluding the year with another visit to Olympia seemed the right thing to do. The weather was just right – cold and crisp – and we were all infused with Christmas spirit. Even though Charlotte had a cold, she rode a beautiful grand prix on Valegro, followed by reprising her Olympic freestyle to win the World Cup qualifier again. While it wasn't their best test, it was a useful wake-up call to remind us that although Valegro's a professor, he is not a machine and still needs riding. So we went into that prize-giving in the top three, with my competitor-friend Isabell Werth of Germany, one of the riders I most respect in the world, in between us.

The Olympic year was done, and Valegro was on top of the world.

Richard Davison *is a seasoned Olympic competitor, and was a member of Team GB for London 2012.*

When we were in London for the final Olympic individual medal class, Carl and I walked together from the warm-up to the main arena. Adelinde Cornelissen had just finished her test, and everyone around the in-gate told us it was fantastic. Carl and I rode every step of Valegro's freestyle, craning our necks and dipping and diving to try to get the best view. There were one or two blips in the test, and bearing in mind what everyone had said about Adelinde's test we turned to each other and consoled ourselves by saying that individual silver was still a dream come true. But a minute or two later, someone leant out of the commentary box situated above the collecting ring area shouting, 'It's gold! Charlotte's got the gold!' It was surreal and it still seems like a dream.

After the Olympics we all went for a few days' break to Sark. It was partly to celebrate, partly to unwind, and also to give the people of Sark a chance to see Carl and share their pride. But it was difficult for everyone close to Valegro, as his sale was now a very real possibility. I remember having a long chat with Charlotte, who was understandably in a whirlwind of emotions. She had just been crowned Olympic champion, but at the same time faced her worst nightmare of losing her beloved partner Valegro.

Isabell Werth (pictured above) has been at the top of dressage sport since her international career began in 1991. Four Olympic, three World and seven European team golds plus her individual titles – Olympic gold in 1996, five European gold medals and three times World Champion – make for a phenomenal international haul. She has also been champion of her native Germany eight times. As the world's most successful dressage rider, Isabell is ideally placed to understand the pressures of not only getting to the top but also staying there.

It is so impressive to see the development of Valegro. I first heard about this new and interesting horse after Vidauban, where he made his grand prix debut, and I first saw him for myself at Rotterdam in 2011. It was really interesting to see this young girl coming in with an easygoing, nothing-to-lose attitude. Then there was Carl with Uthopia, and you could see that with these two super horses the timing was right for the London Olympics. It was just such a super story in the making, the right place, the right time, and the right horses – perfect for great things to happen for Great Britain.

That Charlotte has grown up with Valegro under Carl's wing is great. It is so good that he has been able to be there to guide them step by step, with a really professional team. And Charlotte was strong enough in her mindset to cope with the pressure of expectation – all that 'Will they win? Won't they win? They have to win!' They are a fantastic combination, with Carl behind them as their mentor, taking them by the hand and making sure that everything goes right. The way they work together has been just wonderful to watch.

Charlotte can really ask for top performance from Valegro now, unlike a few years ago when she was a bit unsure: with that experience, they have real routine, and can go out and fight. Of course times like Aachen, where they had mistakes, just show that he is a horse and she is a rider – neither is infallible!

Yes, the time will come when another horse gets closer, but at the moment Valegro is the one to beat. In former times everyone wanted to beat the Germans, then came that really right time in London. The sport should be exciting, not just about one nation. We were asking for a truly global sport and now we have it. It is great for British sport, but more importantly it's great for the sport as a whole. It takes perfect management to bring a horse to the top and keep him there, which shows Carl's immense talent. It is a wonderful story, and it has been fabulous to see it unfold.

Top: They nailed it – Team GBR's first-ever Olympic team medal was the gold, on home ground in London: Carl, Laura Bechtolsheimer and Charlotte wave to the crowds.

Above: The media loved it.

Left: Hugs all round.

Top: Charlotte has her best friend Ian
Cast there to support her.

Above: Hugely proud, Valegro's breeders
Joop and Maartje Hanse were there to see
the Olympic triumph.

Right: Music-maker Tom Hunt with the
golden girl Charlotte.

*Composer and music producer **Tom Hunt** has produced all Valegro's championship freestyles. As Valegro has made his journey to the top, so has Tom, who is now the world's most in-demand composer of dressage freestyles. He also composes for television and film.*

I remember very vividly the first conversation I had with Charlotte. It was spring 2011, and I was on my way back from the gym. As my phone started to ring, I pulled the car over and eagerly looked to see who was calling me. I was expecting the call, but it didn't stop me from being quite excited!

My first musical composition for freestyle dressage was completed for Michael Eilberg in 2010. It was that piece that put me in contact with Rebecca Hughes, who trains with Carl, and was the person who had warned me that I might be getting a call from an up-and-coming British rider called Charlotte Dujardin. Rebecca had passed my number to Charlotte, and I will always be grateful for that. Charlotte needed some freestyle music for the 2011 European Dressage Championships in Rotterdam, and that was the beginning of our musical journey together.

The first time I saw Valegro in the flesh was at Hickstead in 2011, and I was totally in awe of the power and presence he commanded in the ring. Charlotte was riding him in the grand prix, without music obviously, which was a great way for me to focus on Valegro and his movement through the different transitions and paces. I was completely captivated by the way Charlotte and Valegro moved in perfect unison and how easy they made it look. It was hard to believe that they had only just started at grand prix that year.

Musically it has never been difficult to get inspired by a horse like Valegro. When I am working on a freestyle routine, I look at the horse and the way it moves and responds to the rider. I take into account the size and riding style of the horse and where in the test the horse is at its strongest. These are the main areas that I focus on when considering the musical direction. When I started working on Valegro's music, I wanted the music to be big, bold and powerful to support his movement.

Valegro has such a commanding presence, and the music needs to support this. I believe the biggest lesson I have learned from working with him is the importance of musical dynamics in a freestyle test and how to create a musical journey that not only relates to him, but that also captures the imaginations and hearts of spectators.

Valegro is such an exciting horse to watch, and the music needs to highlight this. That first freestyle I worked on for him was a steep learning curve. I was there in Rotterdam and although I was confident with the musical and style choices I had made, I was very apprehensive about how people would react and whether they would be on the 'same page' as I was, especially as this was his first championship music test with Charlotte.

The reality was, it was rather a mixed bag. After Rotterdam it was clear to me that I needed to be much more focused on how to show Valegro off and how to draw on the emotions of his movement through the music. We needed a theme and a clear style that would define this horse.

The music Charlotte and Valegro reprised at Amsterdam in 2014, the *How to Train Your Dragon* theme, was actually first put together for Olympia in 2011. It was at a kind of in-between stage at Olympia, as we were still trying to develop the right musical style after not quite hitting the mark at the Europeans in Rotterdam, but at the same time we had the Olympics coming up in 2012, so the theme was put to one side as we focused on the Olympic music. Two years later, when Charlotte and Carl designed a new floor plan for the World Cup Final in Lyon and the World Equestrian Games in Normandy in 2014, I wanted to go back to the *How to Train Your Dragon* music that we had started looking at back in 2011. This time, however, the focus was to try to keep the musical theme constant throughout, whereas in the 2011 freestyle the test had been made up of different pieces to fill out the programme.

The music for the Olympics was another story. Quite early in 2012 I received a text from Charlotte's best friend Ian Cast, who was over in Hagen supporting her. Valegro had just broken the record for grand prix special, which was obviously fantastic, and I expected Ian's text to be about that, but instead it was about music and a potential thematic direction for Charlotte's next freestyle – the Olympic freestyle, no less!

Ian said that the music playing in the background for Valegro's special at Hagen was the theme from *The Great Escape*, and it had fitted perfectly with Valegro's passage. As soon as Charlotte returned from Germany I received some footage of Valegro working in a few paces including passage, and I began to analyse the movement and rhythm whilst trying the *Great Escape* theme. At first I was a little sceptical that this music had enough power to support Valegro's strength and movement, but the result was just as Ian had described – it looked amazing! I sent Charlotte a short video demo and her response was, 'I love it. It's genius.'

In the few years I'd been working with Charlotte, one thing I had learned was that if you get a response like that from her, then it is definitely worth pursuing! That *Great Escape* theme paved the way for the overall style of the Olympic music, a freestyle celebrating Great Britain and the London Olympics!

Right: That famous 'no rein' exit. Valegro is a humble fellow when it comes to accepting the crowd's appreciation.

Below: 'Good boy, Blueberry!'

6 THE LEGACY OF GOLD

The Rotterdam Championship is a CHIO – a show with Nations Cup competitions in jumping and dressage – and one of Holland's oldest and best-loved sports events. We returned to the Kralingse Bos park, the scene of Valegro's team debut, in June 2013 for his first start of the year. He hadn't competed since the previous December at Olympia, so although he was fit he wasn't as pitch-perfect or competition-tuned as he needed to be, and there were some raw edges. He scored well nonetheless, winning both the grand prix and the freestyle despite not being in perfect self-carriage, and Team GB – Charlotte, Gareth Hughes, Daniel Watson and me – won the team competition. We knew there was a lot to do before the European Championships two months later in Herning in Denmark, but we knew what it was and how to do it.

Previous page and right: Olympia 2012 – another chance for the home fans to see Valegro.

Below: Although there were some mistakes in the freestyle, it was a winning reprise of Valegro's Olympic test.

Opposite, bottom right and left: Tom Hunt created a musical journey that not only relates to Valegro, but also captures the imaginations and hearts of spectators.

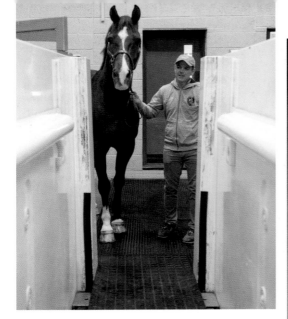

Hickstead in the first few days of August was to be our next and final show before the Europeans. I'd injured my back in a stupid slip downstairs, and was riding hurt, which put a lot of tension in the way of my work, but Valegro's work was going really well and he was looking very fit again. We had started taking both Valegro and Uti to work out on the water treadmill at Hartpury twice a week, which was doing a great job of improving their muscle tone. For the three tests of a championship a horse has to be muscularly fit, and working in the water with no pressure on their back and less on their legs is similar to a human doing a resistance workout in the gym, working core and abs.

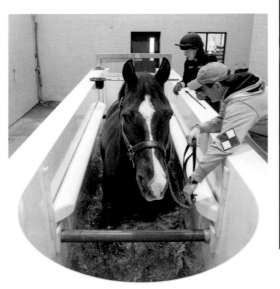

Top left: Alan ushers Valegro into the water treadmill at Hartpury.

Left: Fizz Marshall and Alan supervise Valegro's water treadmill workout.

Fizz and Alan spend many an hour putting the world to rights while Valegro exercises.

Fizz Marshall *MA BSc (Hons) is the Equine Therapy Centre Manager at Hartpury College, where Valegro uses the water treadmill.*

Blueberry has been visiting us here for the last two years as part of his regular exercise routine. He first came along with his stable mate Uthopia. Our Aquafit treadmill is primarily used for mobilisation; the water makes horses sit and drive with the hind legs, whilst off-loading the front legs. It's capable of putting the limbs through their full range of movement, encouraging the horse to elevate his front legs, and flex at the hocks and stifles to keep walking out of the water. Blueberry's movement is so huge that, where most horses would reach their maximal range and start walking through the water as the level comes up, he just keeps lifting his legs higher and higher – I think he would actually kick himself in the tummy if we let him. We provide him with a really good all-over body workout whilst taking the pressure off his legs and feet as part of his normal working week, but particularly in the build-up to shows.

What I feel is more important, however, is what Blueberry does for us. Put simply, we adore him! If he were a person, he would be the most talented athlete you've ever met, but also the most down-to earth-individual on the planet. Like Usain Bolt, but without all the pointing and showing off! As far as he's concerned, when he's here, he's a normal horse and that's what I think I love most. He stands with his head in the office door whilst Alan makes a cup of tea for himself on arrival. He likes Polos, carrots and extra strong mints (but he's less keen on soft mints). He doesn't dance around whilst we get him ready, or make a fuss in any way. The greatest of all the dressage divas in the world is ironically not a diva at all.

On a personal level, Blueberry has given me so much. Firstly he's cemented a friendship that will last a lifetime; Alan and I have spent many hours putting the world to rights standing next to that treadmill. Furthermore, he's propelled my own career forwards by raising the profile of the centre I manage. He has introduced me to two of my heroes, Carl and Charlotte. And, for all of us here, he has made us feel part of something incredible. When you work with horses, your heroes are often not just the riders but the horses themselves, and so the opportunity to meet Valegro has been very special for everyone who has worked here over the last couple of years.

Talking about our work is somewhat odd for us here, as we sign up to very strong confidentiality clauses for every horse we work with. But Carl has talked openly about Uthopia coming to use our water treadmill, and more recently it has become common knowledge that Blueberry is also a frequent visitor. From a business perspective, I cannot state enough what it has done for us. We take less notice of reputation and more of doing as good a job as we can for every case we deal with, but to have the Hester commendation is a wonderful compliment for us and recognises years of work that have gone before.

As members of the general viewing public, we feel fortunate to be part of the Valegro generation; I mean, who doesn't? Will I see another like him in my own lifetime? I wouldn't bet on it. To know him personally, to live the build-up to World Cup finals, World Equestrian Games and Olympics, plus all of the other major shows and championships in between, is a whole other level. We are just a small cog in the wheel, but that doesn't mean we don't cry when he wins or give him huge hugs of good luck and congratulations when he leaves or returns to us after a competition. We love that horse, we are privileged to know him and above all we appreciate his talent, valour and wonderful outlook on life.

Top: Valegro's frequent visits to the
Hartpury water treadmill do wonders
for his fitness and have cemented a great
friendship between Alan and Fizz.

Left: Never any fuss from Valegro.

So off we went to Hickstead in West Sussex. It's a great show, and it's always good to show the horses to the home fans; of course Valegro had many in attendance. The grand prix started brilliantly, and it looked as if we were heading for a new record score. The trot work was brilliant – but the canter? Charlotte had been having a few problems with pirouettes and changes, with Valegro sitting a little too much in the pirouettes and losing momentum, and the changes – well, Charlotte was forgetting to use her legs, and despite Valegro's extraordinary attitude in tests, he's not going to do a movement if he's not asked to. So he missed a beat in a pirouette, and in the one-time changes Charlotte's legs just stopped moving. They still got a wonderful score, but it was just over 80 per cent, not the 85 or 86 it had started out as. Hickstead hosts Britain's sole Nations Cup team competition. There was one grand prix, for both team members and individuals, and then, unusually, the freestyle counted towards the team competition, which I wasn't keen on. It did however work well for us as I was on the team so did the freestyle, while Charlotte, as an individual, did the grand prix special. I had a great freestyle with Uti and we won, whereas Charlotte's special wasn't particularly special, and she was still having those problems in the pirouettes. They might not

have seemed a big deal to anyone else, but we were aiming for perfection, so there was a lot of work to be done and a lot of words to be exchanged before we left for Herning.

Then there was a blow for the team when Laura decided not to take Alf, who wasn't quite 100 per cent, so Gareth Hughes stepped into the breach. But without Alf in attendance, Charlotte and Valegro would have to get a humungous score if GB were going to be in on the team medal haul.

Valegro had changed noticeably in his third year at grand prix: horses usually do as they become more experienced and less 'hot'. He was still keen, of course, as he always is, but he needed a bit more riding. I was not prepared to see those same mistakes again – certainly not in a championship! – and so I gave Charlotte a right 'murdering' during a practice session at Hartpury, where we ran through everything in the music test. Unusually, we went through Valegro's freestyle three times, which is a lot, but while taking care not to put too much pressure on him just before the Europeans, we needed to feel confident that he knew what was being asked of him. The third run-through was spot on, just fabulous. I gave Valegro a sugar lump and sent Charlotte off to do her homework and watch the videos.

'That beautiful face has no comprehension of how good he is.'
(Haydn Price)

Richard Waygood *MBE (pictured above) is the Dressage
Programme Manager at the British Equestrian Federation.
Appointed* chef d'équipe *of the senior British dressage team
in 2010, he was the support bastion for the team during the
London 2012 Olympics and is now working towards Rio 2016.
He was formerly Riding Master of the Household Cavalry
Mounted Regiment, where he used to plan the well-known
Musical Ride. 'Dickie' is one of Britain's most successful
military event riders in recent times, and has competed at
Burghley and Badminton CCI4*s. He is also involved with
training the Team GBR CIC2* eventing team and has many
other coaching, charitable and public-speaking commitments.*

Valegro is the most amazing equine athlete; true and utter
brilliance. Technically he is so correct, and ridden beautifully
by Charlotte: they are a true partnership in every sense. There
are many horses that have talent in abundance, but how
many offer supernatural talent along with an amazing brain
to match this technical ability? If he was an event horse, you
would say he is always looking for the flags – but he's not an
event horse, he is a dressage genius!

One of my lasting memories of this fantastic horse will
be the Europeans in Herning in 2013. Picture the scene – the
lap of honour after the freestyle with 22,000 people standing
and cheering like a Wembley crowd at the FA Cup Final.
Valegro would have got twelves for his extended trot in that
lap of honour, yet the moment he entered the exit tunnel
he broke into walk without so much as a jog step. He was
totally relaxed, with a happy expression on his face as if to
say 'job done'. He has this wonderful ability to know when to
perform, and then to switch off, relax and enjoy a treat from
supremo groom Alan Davies. What a brain!

*Right: The 2013 European Championship
at Herning were held in a football stadium*

*Below: Unanimous verdict in the freestyle
despite the blip*

*Bottom: A much-needed drink for Charlott
– the weight of all those medals*

It was an exciting line-up for the Europeans team, with newcomers Gareth and Michael Eilberg, and although I had a choice of three horses at grand prix, I stuck to the tried and tested Uti, as he had the best chance of a high score. With our brilliant back-up, led by *chef de mission* Will Connell and Dickie Waygood as *chef d'équipe*, it was a fun, focused and on-form team that arrived at Herning in late August for the European Championships.

But the pressure went up a level when poor Gareth had a difficult ride on his mare Nadonna after she took exception to the big screen on the way to the arena, and he had to nurse her through the test. Later that afternoon, Michael and Half Moon Delphi conjured a test with some great moments, but one judge awarded them 8 per cent less than the others. These things happen, and nearly 73 per cent was still a good score, but we were going to have our work cut out to stay in the team medal hunt.

Valegro was working brilliantly, though, and both he and Uti were enjoying themselves. Uti and I had a couple of mistakes, but earned the mark I had expected at 75 per cent. Job done! With Charlotte and Valegro still to come, I felt sure that we were going to be in there somewhere. Helen Langehanenberg rode an amazing test on Damon Hill to put the Germans in gold medal spot, but even then I wasn't nervous for Valegro.

When their turn came, I realised I was standing stock still and just watching every movement, thinking 'yes, yes, yes …' Despite one tiny mistake in the transition from passage to canter, there I was watching the best grand prix I've ever witnessed, and the judges agreed. They posted a world record score of nearly 86 per cent.

The atmosphere was amazing and the suspense palpable, as there was just 1 per cent between the medal-winning nations. Team GB got the bronze, and the colour of the medal didn't matter at all. It was a fantastic competition, with a lot of emotion, and Valegro had broken yet another record. I was so proud of him and of Charlotte, but also of all the medal-winning team members – Germany's gold and Holland's silver – who'd made it on to that podium. As Will Connell said: 'Following the successes of London was always going to be very challenging, but I think that Herning has demonstrated London was certainly not a flash in the pan.' The only downside was that Roly Luard, Valegro's co-owner along with me and now Anne Barrott, arrived ten minutes too late to see Valegro's grand prix.

Of course the individual competitions were all about Valegro. That intense practice at Hartpury had sorted everything and there was an aura of calm surrounding Valegro, Charlotte, Alan and me. That grand prix special was to be outstanding, but unexpectedly it was outstanding for the number of mistakes made. I called it the battle of the dumb blondes when first Sweden's Patrik Kittel and Toy Story went wrong, then Charlotte went wrong when she set off to do her two tempis instead of her canter half-passes! But did it lose them the gold? No, as Helen and Damon Hill promptly went wrong as well, and then Holland's Adelinde and Parzival did exactly the same as Charlotte and Valegro! It was extraordinary, to say the least. But Valegro and Charlotte clinched it with a unanimous first place from the judges (who must have been scratching their heads at all those mistakes) after spectacular work in front of a crowd of some 10,000. And yes, the championships were held in a football stadium!

Left: Spectacular work, even with mistakes.

Top right: As the British national anthem played and Charlotte stood on the podium, Valegro turned to face the Union Jack while Alan stroked his neck.

Bottom right: Alan and Charlotte – big hugs.

Bottom far right: Valegro had done everything he possibly could in that arena.

Andrew Gardner has been a dressage judge for over 25 years. A List 1 judge in Britain, Andrew attained FEI 'O' or 5* status in 2011. He juggles his judging with practising full time as a chartered surveyor, and he officiated at the European Championships in Herning, Denmark, in 2013. He was at B for that error-strewn grand prix special.

The last time I judged Valegro I almost had to pinch myself because of the number of tens that I was awarding. I found I was asking myself, 'What are you doing?' I did wonder how I would compare with my colleagues, but I was not even the highest! This was one of the days where he set a world record – for the kür – but of course he has already broken his own record.

Standing back and thinking about what is a living equine phenomenon, I am struck by the fact that he is free of any controversy. He has purity in his movement and in his way of going; always with such apparent ease but also immense power and lightness too. He is really quite remarkable and I could never have imagined having the good fortune to judge such a universally talented combination so often.

If we think of those areas where he has the ability and often does earn tens, they are at either end of the spectrum: from the powerful extensions to the collection so beautifully presented in half-passes, the piaffe and pirouettes. It is remarkable to have such versatility of talent. He has no weakness.

Besides which, he is just gorgeous in his eye and character. A national and now a world treasure, he is a credit to the equal world talents that are his rider and of course his trainer. The whole team are wonderful; all of them are role models for the future. The sport needs this.

I recall taking a judges' course at the National Championships when Valegro was at a lower level. To this day I remember commenting on his canter and directing my group to observe what I described then as 'world class' potential. At least I got that right! I must say that we judges are privileged to enjoy such wonderful front row seats, but my nerves can't take another championship grand prix special with as many errors as at Herning!

Left: Andrew Gardner.

Right: Valegro, ever the foodie, looks for a taste of Charlotte's flowers.

Below: Charlotte swaps hats with ringmaster Pedro Cebulka: Valegro keeps his own.

It was fortunate that, as Uti and I had finished sixth in the special, there was time for me to be there for Valegro and Charlotte for the freestyle. Again, with that amount of preparation, we knew everything was on track to work. So much so that I said Valegro should have the day before off, which scared Charlotte a little, but I wanted him to be as fresh as possible.

Valegro was completely relaxed, and so was Charlotte. We were expecting it to be the last outing for the Olympic 'Big Ben' freestyle, as Tom Hunt had already prepared the music for a new programme. If it could be perfect, that would be a fitting finale for the Olympic music.

It wasn't quite perfect, with just a little jump in one pirouette when Charlotte caught Valegro with her spur, but everything else, including that final piaffe pirouette, was as near to it as Valegro had ever produced, and the score of 91.25 per cent bagged the gold by nearly 4 per cent. It didn't quite make a record – the only one Valegro had not by then broken – but who cared? The tens came thick and fast, and at the age of eleven Valegro had done everything he possibly could in that arena.

The prize-giving showed just how much this crowd had taken Valegro to their hearts. There were lots of tears, and he loved the atmosphere. As the British national anthem played and Charlotte stood on the podium, Valegro, standing four-square, turned to face the Union Jack while Alan stroked his neck. Being a foodie, though, Valegro did take a munch out of Charlotte's bouquet!

Will Connell is now Director of Sport for the United States Equestrian Federation. From 2003 until after the 2014 World Equestrian Games in Normandy, he was the World Class Performance Director at the British Equestrian Federation. A former commanding officer of the King's Troop, Royal Horse Artillery, Will was leader of the GB equestrian team at the Olympic Games in Athens 2004, Beijing 2008 and London 2012 and chef de mission at the 2006 and 2010 World Equestrian Games. He was responsible for the coordination and delivery of the UK Sport National Lottery funded World Class Programme. In 2012 Will was awarded an MBE in the New Year Honours list in recognition of his services to equestrian sport.

My first memories of Valegro are a little lost in the mists of time, but I remember Carl grabbing me at Windsor and saying I needed to watch the dressage as I would be seeing two horses who'd be in the medals in London – and how right he was. I think that was in 2009, but I can't be sure.

The next time I saw Valegro was in 2011 when Valegro and Charlotte 'came out' at Vidauban in the south of France. It was not an error-free grand prix, but it was the first one for both of them and it was evident to all that something special had just happened. I saw one of GBR's most respected judges at lunch afterwards, and he was in a state of shock. When I asked him what he thought, his response was: 'That was history in the making – one of those special moments that you never forget where you were when it happened.' Judy Harvey and I 'took good wine' to celebrate, while Carl stuck to his mediocre-to-very-poor white plonk; thank heavens he went into dressage and not the wine trade!

That evening I think was the first time I really thought that a shiny team medal at London 2012 was a definite proposition.

Valegro's journey to stardom felt easy, hassle-free and as if the dressage gods had decreed it to be so. Of course there were a few ups and downs and moments of self-doubt behind the scenes, but on the field of play it was a fairytale script become reality. There are many who have helped this journey, but at the heart of it have been Alan, Charlotte, Carl and Roly; together, they have taken dressage to a new level.

So what can I say about the horse? Not a lot really – truly gifted; brain and muscles in the right places; a supreme athlete. Likewise, it is easy to heap praise on Charlotte for all she has achieved; she is the epitome of a gifted athlete with the drive and focus to maximise talent and win when winning is required.

However, the man behind the miracle is Carl. Time and time again, Carl identifies young horses with talent and produces them to Olympic level where they excel. I do not think there has ever been another Olympic gold medal athlete who has coached another athlete to win two golds at the same Games in the same sport or discipline. I cannot find the words that adequately express the respect and admiration I have for Carl as a rider, Carl as a horseman and Carl as a coach.

Left: Carl, 'the man behind the miracle', with Charlotte and Ian Cast after the freestyle in Herning.

Bottom left: Charlotte has had to learn to deal with the media attention.

Below: Will Connell.

Above: Co-owner Roly Luard with Valegro.

Right: Roly Luard and her daughter Bella with Charlotte after London 2012.

Rowena ('Roly') Luard recalls some magical highlights of her co-ownership of Valegro.

Co-owning Valegro has been exciting from the very beginning, when Carl asked me if I would like to buy a half share in him. Valegro was five then, and already winning as he has continued to do.

My memories go back to Rotterdam in August 2011 when Carl did so well on Uthopia – everybody remembers the full set of tens he got for his extended trot. But this was also the first time I was so proud to see Blueberry's name up on the scoreboard. His best placing there was fourth with 78.83 per cent. I was sitting with Jennie Loriston-Clarke, and we could barely contain our excitement.

April 2012 saw us in Hagen, Germany, for the British-themed 'Horses and Dreams'. What an extraordinary competition! To our enormous delight, Valegro won both the grand prix and grand prix special, competing against some up-and-coming superstars. The show was festooned with Union Jack flags and they were on all the merchandise for sale as well. The show background music was from the movie *The Great Escape*, with chimes from Big Ben, and that is where we got the idea of including the chimes in Valegro's freestyle test for the London Olympics.

There were so many wonderful celebrations after winning the gold medals at London 2012. We had already planned a party afloat after the freestyle. We didn't know beforehand if it would be celebration or commiseration, but happily it was the former. None of us on board will ever forget our steamboat sailing under Tower Bridge with the Olympic Rings lit up above us. It was an amazing sight. Then there was the drinks party at Clarence House, and the dinner for all the Olympic equestrians, and Lord Coe's letter of thanks – all these things happened because of Valegro.

The European Championships in Herning the following year was, I think, when Carl and I both realised that we could not entertain the idea of Blueberry being sold and possibly leaving the country. We all had tears in our eyes as he consolidated his place on the world stage.

Of course there were times when I questioned whether Carl was right not to compete Blueberry himself, but I realise now that it all made so much sense. As usual, Carl's plan was the best one. He was to ride Uthopia, and Charlotte was to develop her huge bond with Blueberry, thus helping to form our gold medal winning team.

When Valegro was named KWPN Horse of the Year at Den Bosch in the Netherlands in 2014, what a thrill it was to be standing in the arena with Carl and Blueberry's breeders Joop and Maartje Hanse, while the crowd gave Valegro a massive standing ovation. And then being presented with the Owner of the Year award twice at Olympia – can you imagine it!

Winning the World Cup twice in a lifetime is unimaginable, and for me to be congratulated and welcomed by British Airways on the return flight from Las Vegas in April 2015 illustrates just how wide Valegro's following is.

Above all, the most pleasing thing to see is the enormous bond between horse, rider and trainer, and of course Valegro's bond with Alan, his groom. And then there is Claudine's support and organisational skills and the vets, farriers and physios who are part of all the team events. All of us love Valegro, the horse who never fails to work at his absolute best each time he competes. He never lets us down, but then he is a lucky horse who has had the same team with him throughout his illustrious career. When I think of how we have been supported by Will Connell, Dickie Waygood and Richard Davison, and in the early days Desi Dillingham, and to have the recent interest and support of Anne Barrott and her family too; this bond between all these people has grown over the years and now it's natural – it's our second nature. I am so grateful for the incredible teamwork, and the respect between everyone is really inspiring.

I have made so many lovely new friends through Valegro. Quite simply, he has changed my life.

7 YOU NEVER CAN TELL

It had become a tradition by now to round off the year with a visit to Olympia, and what a landmark that would turn out to be for Valegro in December 2013. There was only one more record to break, that for the freestyle which had been set by Holland's Edward Gal and Totilas in 2009 before Totilas was sold to Germany. Their record – coincidentally set at Olympia – was 92.3 per cent.

Valegro's grand prix wasn't a record-breaker. With a fairly major blip in the canter, he was a little bit tense in his first outing since August, which Charlotte put down to rider error, as was only right. But they still won it decisively by some 4 per cent, ironically from Edward on his rising star Glock's Undercover. Charlotte had that record in her sights, and she wanted it at Olympia, in front of the home fans, but she was well aware that however steely determined she was, it all now depended on what happened in the freestyle.

This really was the last outing for the Big Ben freestyle that had become so iconic a theme for Valegro. You could have heard a pin drop when Valegro entered the arena, and the crowd was rapt. As they got past that left pirouette of the 'Herning blip', Charlotte felt she could breathe again. At 93.975 per cent, they nailed it in front of the home supporters, and the third world record to complete the set was the best Christmas present ever for Charlotte, me and everyone who is part of Valegro's life. Reem Acra, the New York fashion designer who sponsors the FEI World Cup, made this her first visit to a qualifier, and wow, did she pick the right one! Edward was second with Glock's Undercover and characteristically generous on seeing his record broken. 'Valegro is an amazing horse, and Charlotte is a very good rider: I like them both. I always knew that some day it would happen,' he said.

Previous page: Olympia, London − the best possible equestrian Christmas party.

This page: The record of a record being broken. Valegro's fans loved to see him, and the pair scored straight tens for harmony from the judges.

Haydn Price's parents arranged a riding lesson for his twelfth birthday. He was hooked from day one. Two years later, by scrimping and saving every penny, they managed to buy Haydn his first pony. The first time the pony was shod, Haydn became enthralled by the art and craft of farriery. By the second shoeing, he had already decided farriery would be his career, and he hasn't looked back since. After graduating with the Worshipful Company of Farriers in 1983, Haydn went on to develop a farriery business specialising in shoeing performance horses. Haydn is consultant farrier to the British Equestrian Federation, and team farrier to the British dressage and show jumping teams, as well as being a regular contributor to publications and research programmes and an international lecturer.

First of all there is the impression the public get. For example, in the run-up to the London Olympics I was asked for lots of interviews, and during one long one for the *American Farriers' Journal* I was asked whether Valegro was my favourite horse. Well, everyone assumes he'd be top of the list because of what he's achieved, but it's his personality that exceeds everything else. As a 'person' he is very special and he's very humble.

The memory that stands out for me is not his tests, but when he walks out of the arena. It is as if he's saying, 'Thanks for coming, thank you for watching.' That beautiful face has no comprehension of how good he is. So outside the arena he is 'Bob the cob', he's my mate.

With my hand on my heart I can honestly say he's not treated any differently. When it comes to being shod, he's brought out, trotted up, then tied up outside. But he can second-guess which foot I want, and he'll just pick up each one without being asked.

In Normandy I was at the prize-giving with my wife and some friends. As Alan turned him to face the audience, just tickling the back of his neck for reassurance, the crowd went wild for that horse. Valegro has such empathy; he's the sort of person you'd imagine you could slot in the middle if you had your mother and the vicar to tea! He is just a lovely person.

Clockwise from left: 'No foot, no horse,' goes the saying – farrier Haydn Price keeps Valegro's toes in top condition.

Forging the designer shoes.

Carefully shaping those special feet.

The dogs gather round – all partial to a bit of toenail as Ryan McDonald, Haydn's apprentice, does the preliminary trim.

That Valegro was being put up for sale after the Olympics was common knowledge. That was the agreement in place between Roly and me, and we'd done it before with my Athens Olympics star Escapado (now happily enjoying retirement with Caroline Dawson, who had looked after him so brilliantly), as this was part of the deal. Hard as it is, there is always practicality to consider if you're not a multi-millionaire. But after everything Valegro had given us and his country, could we go through with it? Could we let go of his lifestyle and the way he'd been brought up – and could anyone else replicate them? In the end, we decided that we couldn't and they couldn't. I just wasn't going to be mortgage free, that was all. When we announced this decision after Olympia, and *Horse & Hound* published a story in early January 2014 to say we wanted to syndicate Valegro, who'd have thought

that this would be the catalyst for his new co-owner to join us on this amazing journey?

Anne Barrott, who contacted Roly after that story was published, hadn't been involved with dressage before, and like me she isn't from a horsey background, but with a big desire to see Valegro stay in this country she stepped in, and we're delighted to have her as part of Team Valegro.

It took a while to sort out, but Valegro's future was secure. Of course this was a huge relief to Charlotte, who had obviously taken the possibility of Valegro's sale very hard, but 2014 was all about moving on – and up!

With the European and Olympic titles in the bag, the one remaining set of gold medals and titles left to win were the World Championship ones. And at least we didn't have a long way to go to Caen, in Normandy.

Left: Valegro with his owners Roly Luard, Anne Barrott and Carl Hester.

Below: Valegro — trusting in his family.

*Amid the furore over Valegro's possible sale after victory at the London 2012 Olympics, **Anne Barrott** became the third member of the Valegro syndicate in 2014. Anne did not have a dressage background, and her willingness to step into the breach is just another fascinating part of the Valegro story.*

I always get *Horse & Hound* so, after the Olympics, I was reading all these stories about Valegro being up for sale, but time went on and nothing happened. It has always irritated me that these elite horses do so well and are then are sold abroad and never heard of again.

I'm not 'horsey' myself, and only got involved as my daughter Julia, who has since gone on to two-star eventing, got keen at the age of eight. It went on from there to a breeding programme and me learning to ride in my forties!

A bit later, in January 2014 after Olympia, there was another piece in *Horse & Hound* saying that Valegro was no longer for sale, and instead a syndicate would be formed. I thought that sounded like a good idea and asked *Horse & Hound* to pass on my details to Roly and Carl, neither of whom I knew then.

My first visit to Carl's yard was in May 2014. I'd put my hand up to become a co-owner and found myself coming in right at the top of the dressage world – it was surreal. It was summer by the time all the details were sorted out, and Valegro was going to the World Equestrian Games in Normandy, but I was already committed elsewhere so Julia went instead.

My first show as co-owner was Olympia in December 2014, which was really going in at the deep end, but wonderful of course, with Amsterdam soon after in January. Charlotte threw her bouquet to me in Amsterdam as she brought Valegro back to the stables. He was far more interested in that than in me! I don't know him very well yet, but I quickly gathered he likes his food.

What struck me first is how laid-back he is. In Las Vegas in April 2015, Julia and I went to see him in the stables and found him being plaited up. There was Alan on his step-ladder, working away, while Valegro – with no headcollar on, not tied up – just stood there. He is very chilled. And then after such magnificent tests Charlotte drops the reins on his neck and he just ambles out of the arena, looking at the crowd as if to say, 'You liked it, then?'

Having bred horses that are now aged seventeen and nineteen, I do know, even without being 'horsey', about that understanding that comes from knowing everything about them, knowing where they came from. And Valegro has had his family around him from a very young age. I know everyone was worried about him in Vegas, but when I saw him he was much more perky. It struck me that when Carl and Charlotte arrived he felt better now that his family were all there. It's all about trust, and now he even puts up with me! I will always be there for him if I can. It is lovely to be the third name on his passport.

Left: Valegro's new floor plan for Lyon added new technical difficulty, including changes on curved lines.

Right: The engine that produced that remarkable extended trot.

With that freestyle record, it made sense to go for the World Cup Final with Valegro. Charlotte and Valegro would have to be in the top eight in the Western European League to qualify for the final, so after Christmas, while Charlotte was away in New Zealand doing some clinics, I took over Valegro's reins in the run-up to the second qualifier he'd need to do, in Amsterdam in January. Charlotte returned two days before the show, complete with jet lag. I obviously didn't do a bad job, as the grand prix was just 0.122 per cent lower than the Herning record-breaking test, and the freestyle was an exercise in pure Valegro professorship. With a new programme under way and due to be showcased at the Final, we decided to use the first freestyle that Tom Hunt had created for Valegro. It was atmospheric, relaxed and harmonious, and looked easy, as had by then become the combination's trademark. There was just one little mistake in the two tempis when a camera flash uncharacteristically startled Valegro, but they still posted over 91 per cent, 6 per cent ahead of Edward Gal and Glock's Undercover. So then it was back to home and normality for Valegro before his and Charlotte's first FEI World Cup Final in the historic French city of Lyon, where they would come up against defending title-holders Helen Langehanenberg and Damon Hill.

Well, I say normality, but on 3 April, two weeks before Lyon, Valegro was 'sat on' by a certain well-known young lady who came to meet him on her birthday as a special treat. Lots of people come to our open days and love meeting the wonder horse, and of course Blueberry is always on his best behaviour for them. It was news to me that Leona Lewis, the most successful *X-Factor* winner ever, was both a rider and a dressage fan, but she came to see Valegro on her birthday. She loved meeting him, and we loved meeting her. She is gorgeous, and she nearly got Valegro 'on the bit'. And I loved it when the Hollywood celebrity blogger Perez Hilton wrote about Leona's visit: 'So she must've been ecstatic when she got to ride an Olympic gold medalist's horse!! On her birthday too! That's so great. That's so cool! We bet she was totally in heaven.' It's moments like these that remind me how special this smallish, squat horse that I saw all those years ago is – and I'd have been an idiot to let him go, as I said to the Dutch audience during that Rotterdam European Championships! I think Leona really was smitten, because later in April she came to watch Valegro in Lyon, when Charlotte became the first Briton ever to win the World Cup Final, on their first outing with the new freestyle that Tom Hunt had patiently worked on for so long.

The freestyle music, from the Dreamworks animated film *How to Train Your Dragon*, is now famous and was awaited then with much anticipation. Charlotte had only ridden through it twice before, and of course wasn't completely confident with it, but all the movements worked. It was a much more technically difficult floor plan. We had added curved lines for the changes and extended canter to double pirouette on the centre lines, plus a difficult piaffe pirouette at the end. Valegro was just a star, and I loved watching him to the new music which complemented his paces and the drama of the programme so brilliantly.

It's always a pressure to come from a calm warm-up arena to such a huge atmosphere, and some horses can change in 30 metres in that situation – but with Valegro being such a professor, he doesn't. (We have called him 'professor' for years, as he seemed to have read every book about dressage before he even started.) Charlotte can always feel safe that what she gets in the warm-up, she can get in the ring, and by now I felt safe watching them.

Helen Langehanenberg and Damon Hill, in second place, made a couple of mistakes, and Edward coped with a rather excited Glock's Undercover for third. Charlotte and Valegro, in front of a full house, now had a full set of dressage titles.

With the World Games in Caen coming up, but not until August, it seemed the groundwork was laid. We never go to many competitions during the year, and 2014 was no exception. Valegro had three months of his normal home routine, and then one final outing planned before Normandy.

Top: 'The Professor' in action.

Left: Carl felt safe watching Valegro and Charlotte.

*Lyon 2014: the first British combination
ever to win the Dressage World Cup.*

Marnie Campbell *(née Malgarin), one of the UK's leading equine sports therapists, has been Valegro's physiotherapist since he was five. His fortnightly massages from her are his favourite thing after food.*

Valegro became one of my favourite clients from the beginning, even before he was famous. He was always a very special person, and I see a lot of horses every day, including Gold Cup winning racehorses and other very good sport horses. But Valegro, although he knows he's successful, is so kind, so knowing. He is an old soul. I think he has an aura about him which makes him very special to be with. If he were a person, he'd be the star who never gets above his station, who stays grounded. Alan and I have agreed we will never see another horse like him in our lifetimes.

I see Valegro every two weeks, and he absolutely loves his hour of massage. He goes to sleep, but even if he's having a treatment, if he wants a drink I have to untie him and let him do it – that's the only remotely diva-like behaviour he ever shows.

I don't go to all the shows, but at the World Equestrian Games in Normandy in 2014 it struck me how happy Valegro was to be at the show. He's happy at home, but he comes alive at a show – it's as if he lights up.

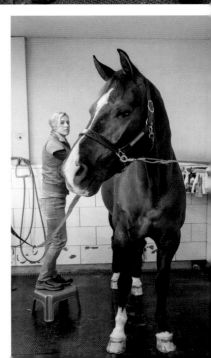

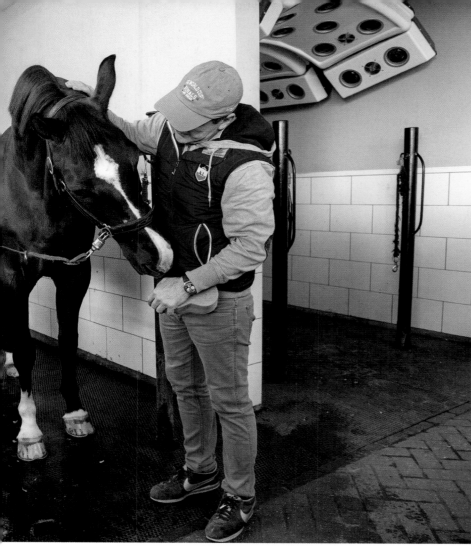

Marnie at work with her magic hands.

Watching Fiona during a post-work solarium session.

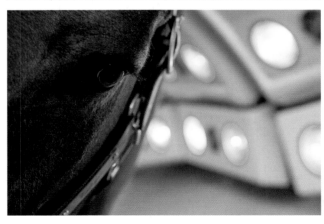

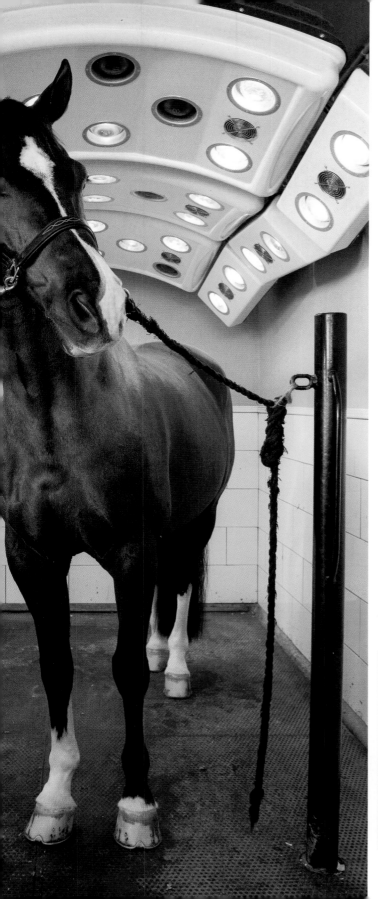

A day in the life of a champion horse –
valet service from Alan.

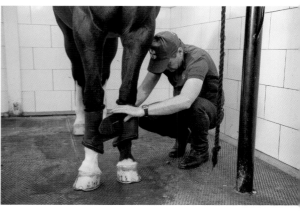

Aachen CHIO is known as the biggest show on earth. With jumping, eventing, displays, shopping and eateries, it's full of atmosphere and huge crowds. The dressage crowd there is knowledgeable, and it is *the* show for seeing champions in action, as it is a Nations Cup team competition even when it is not hosting the championship of the year. Winning the Aachen Championships – in both dressage and jumping – is as coveted a prize as any, and this was billed as a 'mini World Championships' before the real one a few weeks later in Caen. Although Charlotte had made her Aachen debut in 2011 on her own horse, Fernandez, this would be her debut at the German show with Valegro.

And it was there that the wheels came off. I never underestimate the pressure Charlotte is under with Valegro: the expectations are massive. Helen and Damon Hill (Dami) were in the field along with Isabell Werth on her rising star Bella Rose, as well as Matthias Rath and Totilas, who looked as if he had returned to form with a nearly fault-free grand prix test. Helen and Dami made a few mistakes but seemed to be heading off Totilas until a major blip on the last centre when Dami ground to a halt in the final passage.

Charlotte and Valegro started, and it all looked on form until the canter. Mistakes, mistakes, mistakes; in the changes, the zigzag, the pirouettes – I couldn't believe what I was seeing. Sixth place on 76 per cent! But what it meant was simple: Valegro is a real horse and Charlotte is human. It was almost a relief to see it, and while some people were surprised that I wasn't upset with Charlotte, at that time what she really needed was support. Sure, we were disappointed in the test, but how could I ever be disappointed in Charlotte? How could I ever be disappointed in Valegro? I couldn't. We just had some work to do.

Testing times at Aachen 2014, and Alan's face says it all.

For the special, things went better – still some mistakes in the changes, and a couple of blips, but Charlotte and Valegro were second to Totilas, with Helen and Damon Hill in front of the much-admired Bella Rose, who looked fabulous for Isabell Werth. The weather was incredibly hot, nearly 35 degrees, I think, and we had to ask ourselves whether Valegro needed to be fitter, and had the warm-up been too long? It was a steep learning curve, but an essential one.

Valegro was on the uphill curve for the final freestyle and, despite making more uncharacteristic mistakes in the changes, they won the class and the championship – the first time a British combination had won the Aachen main prize since Joan Gold and Gay Gordon in 1958. But it has to be said their victory was in the absence of Totilas, who had been withdrawn. As I said in my *Horse & Hound* column at the time, I wasn't sure whether this move was tactful or tactical, but the whole event just made the prospect of the forthcoming World Equestrian Games in Caen even more exciting.

Team GB for the World Equestrian Games took the same form as the previous year. Michael, who had broken the 80 per cent barrier with Half Moon Delphi at Aachen; Gareth and Nadonna; me with Nip Tuck who was making his team debut; and of course Charlotte and our professor, who had been doing a bit of revision. Just like before the Europeans, we had to reassess where we were and where we wanted to be. Charlotte and Valegro had been a partnership for eight years and they knew each other inside out, but grand prix is not a static stage of training, and Aachen's wake-up call was a timely reminder of that. As with any virtuoso performers, when communication between horse and rider is at this level of finesse, it's the fine-tuning that matters. Valegro needed the girl on top to give him some direction, and Charlotte needed to sharpen up and not expect it all to happen. She'd never felt Valegro as worried in a test as he was in that Aachen grand prix – he simply wasn't used to making mistakes. But of course it made her more determined than ever as she went into her first-ever World Equestrian Games.

Even after the loss of Totilas through injury, the German team was at full strength: Isabell and Bella Rose, Helen and Damon Hill and Kristina Sprehe with Desperados were unbeatable in gold position, with an average score of over 80 per cent. It was all on Charlotte and Valegro's shoulders to claim the silver. They needed some 81 per cent, and they nailed it with a comfortable 4 per cent margin. The only setback was an early halt on the start centre line (which, weirdly, Damon Hill did too), but it didn't matter, as Valegro was back at the top of the leader board. We'd gone in with realistic hopes of bronze. Silver was a shining bonus.

We were all saddened by Bella Rose's withdrawal through lameness. Isabell is a great competitor, and I was looking forward to seeing more of her wonderful mare who'd broken the 80 per cent barrier to come second in the grand prix. I am sure I will in time, but that year in Normandy – well, that was horses for you, and rotten luck too.

After that, Charlotte was confident for the first of the two individual tests, but telling the media 'any medal will do' wasn't quite the whole truth. That Valegro scored over 86 per cent despite three silly mistakes just shows how brilliant the rest of the work was. He is not a machine, and he needed the loo during a piaffe, and for once Charlotte found the crowd distracting as they volubly expressed their surprise at the mistakes – she wanted to turn round and say 'Shut up!' But because she thought those mistakes had cost her the gold, she asked for a bit more from Valegro to try to catch up, and he just gave it, and earned his third grand prix special championship.

The freestyle, only the third time Valegro had performed the *How to Train Your Dragon* programme in competition, was spectacular. There was a roar from the 20,000-strong crowd as Valegro and Charlotte entered the arena, but that did not unsettle them. Each had confidence in the other, and they went out to have fun and didn't think about the pressure. With a score just 1.8 per cent shy of their Olympia freestyle record, Charlotte become the first dressage rider ever to hold the Olympic, European and World titles at the same time. Silver in both tests went to Germany's Helen Langehanenberg and Damon Hill, while Holland's Adelinde Cornelissen on Parzival snatched the bronze from the third-placed combination in the special, Germany's Kristina Sprehe and Desperados. It was an amazing event, even though the food provided for humans on the showground was ghastly. Fortunately Valegro's wasn't – he'd brought his own!

Fun and confidence all the way through to the prize-giving for the new World Champions.

Carl's long-term friend and team-mate **Richard Davison** had been on the London 2012 team with Carl and Charlotte. He recalls the seesaw events of 2014 at Aachen and Caen.

Shortly before the 2014 World Equestrian Games, Carl had entered Charlotte and Valegro in Aachen. It had not got off to a good start, with Charlotte and Valegro making numerous uncharacteristic mistakes and suffering from a lack of focus. Over the three tests they gradually got better and won the overall title. But it created doubt in many peoples' minds – had the bubble burst, and had they reached their peak?

Next time out was WEG (the World Equestrian Games), and as I sat by myself watching the warm-up arena where Charlotte and Valegro were training under Carl's tuition, if I had any doubts they rapidly evaporated. I was mesmerised by what I saw, and I wrote in my *Horse & Hound* report: 'The evening before their team test, I was transfixed watching Charlotte training Valegro. They were producing this alchemy of energy, harmony and correctness, and I recall telling myself that Valegro is simply the best dressage horse the world has ever seen.' A few moments later, the full meaning of those words dawned on me, and from then on I never doubted that Charlotte and Valegro would be crowned World Champions.

Above: Caen 2014, Normandy World Championships.

Right: Oh no… Oh no! Oh YES!

Lucinda Green *MBE (pictured above) is an eventing legend. The six-times Badminton winner and former World and European champion had the chance to ride Valegro for one of her 'Lucinda rides' articles for* Horse & Hound *magazine.*

It was after Valegro and Charlotte had become European Champions, at the beginning of the Olympic year, that I headed to Gloucestershire to ride Valegro.

His walk felt lovely, but as we went into trot it was like sitting on an entirely different species to anything I have ever ridden – soft, smooth, yet every bit of his body moving, and so soft in his back that he was surprisingly easy to sit to – that is, until I first tried medium trot! Then Valegro produced so much power he nearly bounced me out of the saddle and I got the giggles. But Carl's advice to sit 'as though sitting on a trampoline' was on the mark.

What a canter! And flying changes – I only had to think of them for them to happen. I rode Valegro in a rubber snaffle, with no whip and no spurs, yet he produced this wonderful expression. He is such a sensitive ride in the best possible way. I compared it at the time to driving a small Ferrari when you're used to a Mini Metro, and the smile on my face said it all. It was so much fun and as big a thrill as jumping a massive fence.

Valegro was such a wonderful, kind, giving horse that just for those magic fifteen minutes I liked dressage and did not feel completely unable to do it.

Once again, giving Valegro's British fans a chance to see him at Olympia that year was a must. We never go to shows thinking about setting world records, let alone breaking the records Valegro and Charlotte have already set, but that's what happened here, in both the grand prix and the freestyle. For the grand prix they scored 87 per cent, and for the freestyle, 94.3 (breaking their own record by over 3 per cent). They were awarded straight tens for harmony, and that is the secret: it is all about partnership. The partnership that Charlotte and Valegro have developed over eight years together is rooted in trust and an intimate knowledge of each other's strengths and weaknesses. That's what enables these performances of sheer confidence and brilliance. Valegro is innately a worker, both inside and outside the arena. Charlotte knows that what you can get from him at home you can also get in the arena, and that is what gives her the confidence to ask for more, knowing Valegro will always give it.

Trond Asmyr (pictured above with Charlotte and Valegro) is Director of Dressage and Para-Equestrian Dressage at the FEI. He has been a judge for more than 30 years, and an international 'I' judge for fifteen. Trond was also on the board of directors for the Norwegian Equestrian Federation and served as its vice president for six years before joining the FEI in 2009.

Sometimes in life you get the feeling that something is perfect, and that's what I feel when I see Valegro and Charlotte dancing around the arena. As an FEI person, I see this as the perfect illustration of the objectives of dressage according to our rules: developing the horse into a happy athlete, through harmonious education, and achieving perfect understanding with the athlete.

Valegro has brought dressage up to a level we have never seen before. Of course having all three world records is a sign of this, but to me it is also the fact that he has become a world star through his charisma. He 'owns the stage' and obviously loves it. He really rises to the occasion.

We know it is important to attract young people to dressage. When I see the long queues of young girls lining up to get Charlotte's autograph, it is so impressive, and to me this is a good sign of what Valegro and Charlotte mean for the sport.

For me as a dressage judge, it would be a dream come true to judge them and give all those tens they so richly deserve. The record is now more than 95 per cent, so there is still room for many new records before we reach the ceiling.

Left and bottom left: On the way to delivering a perfect Christmas present.

Below: Alan accompanies Charlotte and Valegro to the prize-giving at the best equestrian Christmas party.

Olympia is the best possible equestrian Christmas party, and to end the year with those records and those scores was another perfect Christmas present for all of us who work with and love Valegro. The music seemed more emotive than ever, and Charlotte had to bite her lip to hold back her tears as she and Valegro finished their freestyle. The crowd gave them a standing ovation as Valegro strolled nonchalantly out of the arena towards a waiting Alan while Charlotte hugged his neck and waved to his fans.

Left: Olympia 2014, and another record smashed – Charlotte and Valegro's own freestyle.

Below: Another interview for Charlotte.

That's what Valegro does, and that's what he did again a few months later in Las Vegas. Is there more to come? Nothing's certain, of course, but we wouldn't bet against it. As far as making plans and predictions goes, what can I say? He has broken every record and holds every title. Rio 2016 is the aim for Valegro and Charlotte to defend their Olympic title, with the European Championships in Aachen a year before. As long as Valegro is happy competing, he can go on doing so. He loves meeting his fans, and the looks on their faces when they meet him are priceless. He has made Charlotte's name as a rider. Perhaps most memorably, he has put British dressage on the map and made the British way of training the most admired in the world for the harmony that it achieves between horse and rider. That harmony is what all up-and-coming riders now aspire to.

For his owners (me, Roly Luard and now Anne Barrott), for everyone who looks after him (and especially Alan), for Charlotte, and for everyone who knows and loves him, he has changed our lives and touched our hearts. To Valegro, our Blueberry, our Professor, thank you for being you.

Below: Valegro loves nothing more than being in the field, eating.

Bottom: As long as Valegro is happy competing, he can go on doing so.

Above: Valegro has made Charlotte's name as a rider.

Left: Meeting some delighted young fans sporting their Valegro t-shirts.

Claire Hester is a longstanding friend of Carl's from his early days on Sark in the Channel Islands, as well as a family member through marriage and now his near neighbour in Gloucestershire. She owns Weidyfleur II, Valegro's full sister, who is creating a legacy via the bloodlines she shares with Valegro. Like Valegro, Weidyfleur II was bred by the Hanses, and she was born the year after her brother. Originally she was not for sale but, as with Valegro, she was secured by Gertjan van Olst, who sent her to Carl, who then sold her in turn to Claire when she set up her own breeding operation.

Weidyfleur II, known as Marey at home, is a lovely mare and I was lucky to be able to buy her before Valegro got really famous. I adore her, as I do her offspring. She was never ridden and has spent her life as a broodmare. Weidyfleur did her first testing in Holland, and has a PROK predicate (essentially a high radiological score, indicating her suitability for breeding). Weidyfleur is like Valegro in that she carries a lovely top line; her neck positioning, head type and set and quarters are powerful, and she is similar to him in her leg structure too. She throws big foals with lots of bone.

U-Genius (known as Douglas at home, and previously registered as Euphoria) was the first foal she had with me. By Uthopia, he was born in 2011 before we knew that Valegro and Uthopia would be on the same Olympic team. He was quite an ugly duckling and, rather like Valegro in his younger days, most people were quick to dismiss him. I have kept him quietly at home, making sure he had the best care and nutrition, while letting him have a very relaxed and happy first few years in the field. He has matured beautifully and now, at four, has grown into a very handsome and well-proportioned horse with a lot of similar traits to both Valegro and Uthopia. He has a very good, 'no-nonsense', clever brain, fantastic power, super movement and undeniable presence.

It is my aim to keep him a stallion so we can start to build on the best bloodlines Britain has, and so far, so good – he seems to be able to concentrate on his ridden work and control his power even when spring is in the air. I haven't rushed to put him in four-year-old classes, as I wanted to give him time to mature at his own pace and not be faced with mares being ridden in the same arena while he is still such a 'teenager'. I sent him to stud early, at two and a half, for semen to be collected and frozen just in case he was too 'hot' to keep a stallion. He will be covering a very nice mare this season, so I hope the first grand-progeny of Valegro and Uthopia will be born next year. I'll keep U-Genius for the long haul and, fingers crossed, he will emulate both his father and his uncle.

Weidyfleur II has bred a further three foals; a filly by Lord Leatherdale, followed by a colt (Integro) by Dimaggio, and on 5 May 2015 a lovely filly by Uthopia from embryo transfer was born, a full sister to U-Genius, ensuring the 'Olympic' line continues through the all-important dam line. All are gorgeous and maturing nicely. Again they are growing up quietly at home until they are ready for their first public outings. It's exciting to see these bloodlines are continuing.

U-Genius was first backed aged two and a half as he was big and so that he would be easier to handle when he first went to stud. Tessa Clarke at West Kington stud had been dubious about taking such a baby for 'practice' stud duties, but she phoned me the day after he arrived to tell me how much she loved him and how easily he had taken to it all. When he arrived at the stud he was stabled next to Chilli Morning (the eventing stallion who won team silver and individual bronze with William Fox-Pitt at the 2014 World Equestrian Games, and in 2015 was the first stallion to win Badminton) and we couldn't help laughing as they leant towards each other over the stable doors, as if Chilli was passing on a few stallion secrets! Now that U-Genius is a four-year-old, we've recently re-backed him and I've spent a lot of time with him at home, starting him slowly, long-reining with lots of transitions to build up his core strength, so his power doesn't overtake his maturity. Amy Woodhead, very talented and one of Carl's future stars, rides him for me at home and Carl is very enthusiastic about the prospect of taking over the reins at the next stage – U-Genius is, after all, the direct progeny of his two Olympic stars, and Carl says this is the last horse he will take to grand prix – and what a fitting end to this extraordinary story that would be!

Top: Weidyfleur II, Valegro's sister, and her foal, now called U-Genius.

Above: Claire Hester with Valegro's nephew Integro (at left) and Incognito, also bred by her.

Right: Amy Woodhead riding U-Genius.

Demonstrating the British way of training – all about harmony.

Carl, Charlotte and Valegro: 'It is a wonderful story, and it has been fabulous to see it unfold.' (Isabell Werth.)

It's gold! Carl and the team applaud another triumph – World Equestrian Games, Caen 2014.

VALEGRO'S MAJOR EVENTS AND RESULTS

INTERNATIONAL CHAMPIONSHIPS

European Championships, Rotterdam 2011	Team gold
Olympics, London 2012	Team gold
	Individual gold
European Championships, Herning 2013	Team bronze
	Individual gold (grand prix special and freestyle)
Lyon 2014	FEI World Cup
World Equestrian Games, Caen 2014	Team silver
	Individual gold (grand prix special and freestyle)
Las Vegas 2015	FEI World Cup

OTHER INTERNATIONAL AWARDS

February 2013	KWPN Horse of the Year

NATIONAL CHAMPIONSHIPS

Date	Class	Rider
July 2006	Badminton Young Dressage Horse of the Future	Lucy Cartwright
September 2006	Shearwater Four-Year-Old Champion	Carl Hester
July 2007	Badminton Young Dressage Horse of the Future	Carl Hester
September 2007	Shearwater Five-Year-Old Champion	Charlotte Dujardin
September 2007	Novice Champion	Charlotte Dujardin
April 2008	Winter Elementary Champion	Charlotte Dujardin
September 2008	Shearwater Six-Year-Old Champion	Charlotte Dujardin
September 2008	Elementary & Medium Champion	Charlotte Dujardin
April 2009	Winter Advanced Medium Champion	Charlotte Dujardin
September 2010	Prix St George & Intermediaire I Champion	Charlotte Dujardin

FEI (INTERNATIONAL EQUESTRIAN FEDERATION) RECORD

Start date	Show	Event	Competition	Position	Score %
19 March 2011	Vidauban	CDI3*	GP	1	73.723
25 March 2011	Vidauban	CDI3*	GPS	1	74.667
27 March 2011	Vidauban	CDI3*	GP	1	73.396
28 April 2011	Saumur	CDI3*	GP	2	73.340
30 April 2011	Saumur	CDI3*	GPS	1	73.854
24 June 2011	Fritzens	CDI4*	GP	1	77.979
26 June 2011	Fritzens	CDI4*	GPS	2	76.292
30 July 2011	Hickstead	CDI5*	GP	3	78.255
31 July 2011	Hickstead	CDI5*	GPS	1	76.604
17 August 2011	Rotterdam	CH-EU	Final classification	6	
18 August 2011	Rotterdam	CH-EU	GP	4	78.830
20 August 2011	Rotterdam	CH-EU	GPS	6	76.548
21 August 2011	Rotterdam	CH-EU	GP FS	9	79.357
14 December 2011	London Olympia	CDI-W	GP	1	81.043
15 December 2011	London Olympia	CDI-W	GP FS	2	83.700
27 January 2012	West Palm Beach, Florida	CDI4*	GP	2	78.468
28 January 2012	West Palm Beach, Florida	CDI4*	GP FS	2	83.650
27 April 2012	Hagen	CDI4*	GP	1	81.426
29 April 2012	Hagen	CDI4*	GPS	1	88.022
6 July 2012	Hartpury	CDI3*	GP	1	81.660
7 July 2012	Hartpury	CDI3*	GP FS	1	90.650
2 August 2012	London	Olympic Games	Final classification	1	
3 August 2012	London	Olympic Games	GP	1	83.663
7 August 2012	London	Olympic Games	GPS	1	83.286
9 August 2012	London	Olympic Games	GP FS	1	90.089
17 December 2012	London Olympia	CDI-W	GP	1	84.447
18 December 2012	London Olympia	CDI-W	GP FS	1	87.975
20 June 2013	Rotterdam	CDIO5*	GP	1	82.191
22 June 2013	Rotterdam	CDIO5*	GP FS	1	87.425

Start date	Show	Event	Competition	Position	Score %
2 August 2013	Hickstead	CDIO3*	GP	1	81.660
4 August 2013	Hickstead	CDIO3*	GPS I	1	85.000
19 August 2013	Herning	CH-EU-D	Final classification	1	
22 August 2013	Herning	CH-EU-D	GP	1	85.942
23 August 2013	Herning	CH-EU-D	GPS	1	85.699
24 August 2013	Herning	CH-EU-D	GP FS	1	91.250
16 December 2013	London Olympia	CDI-W	GP	1	84.851
17 December 2013	London Olympia	CDI-W	GP FS	1	93.975
24 January 2014	Amsterdam	CDI-W	GP	1	85.820
25 January 2014	Amsterdam	CDI-W	GP FS	1	91.275
19 April 2014	Lyon	CDI-W Final	GP	1	87.129
20 April 2014	Lyon	CDI-W Final	GP FS	1	92.179
17 July 2014	Aachen	CDIO5*	GP	6	76.900
19 July 2014	Aachen	CDIO5*	GPS	2	83.157
20 July 2014	Aachen	CDIO5*	GP FS	1	87.900
24 August 2014	Caen	WEG	Final classification	1	
26 August 2014	Caen	WEG	Team competition (qualifier for individual)	1	85.271
27 August 2014	Caen	WEG	GPS	1	86.120
29 August 2014	Caen	WEG	GP FS	1	92.161
16 December 2014	London Olympia	CDI-W	GP	1	87.460
17 December 2014	London Olympia	CDI-W	GP FS	1	94.300
30 January 2015	Amsterdam	CDI-W	GP	1	86.140
31 January 2015	Amsterdam	CDI-W	GP FS	1	93.900
16 April 2015	Las Vegas	CDI-W Final	GP	1	85.414
17 April 2015	Las Vegas	CDI-W Final	GP FS	1	94.196
10 July 2015	Hartpury	CDI3*	GP	1	85.440
12 July 2015	Hartpury	CDI3*	GPS	1	87.765

Key

CDI: International Dressage Competition

CH-ED: European Championships

GP: Grand Prix

GP FS: Grand Prix Freestyle to Music

GPS: Grand Prix Special

WEG: World Equestrian Games

PICTURE CREDITS

Valegro at home, in the field beside Carl's house.

INDEX

Page references for illustrations appear in *italic*

Note: As Carl Hester, Charlotte Dujardin and Valegro himself are present throughout, they are not specifically listed in the index.

Alan chatting to Valegro: 'He's a great listener and will always put a smile on your face.'